THE GUITAR CHORD SHAPES
OF
Charlie CHRISTIAN

by Joseph Weidlich

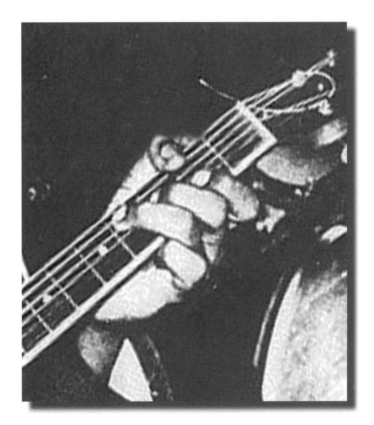

Photo's courtesy of Leo Valdes, http://home.elp.rr.com/valdes/
Music Notation-Randy Ames
Layout-Dave Collins
Production-Ron Middlebrook

Editors notes: The CD musical tracks were not played on
a guitar but generated from the music program.

ISBN   1-57424-149-4
SAN   683-8022

TABLE OF CONTENTS

It has often been stated in various books and articles on jazz guitarist Charlie Christian that he often played, i.e., improvised, "out of chord shapes." This makes sense since Swing Era bands were noted for playing riffs on various scale degrees; if those riffs are played on the guitar out of a chord shape they are then moveable, thus one can play them in virtually any key without difficulty by simply moving the shape up or down the fingerboard. As the use of the concert keys of A flat and D flat (having key signatures of four and five flats respectively) were not unusual, i.e., user friendly keys for the brass instruments (but not for the guitar!), it is important to remember that those keys are only a half-step removed from the more common guitar keys of D and A. Learn the riffs in those keys and all you have to then do is move the shape up or down one fret and you will then be playing in those flat keys. This was just one of the elements of Charlie Christian's genius in making the guitar a *bona fide* solo instrument in the jazz ensemble.

The purpose of this book is to present some of the common licks often used by Charlie Christian in the basic chord shapes of F, D and A, i.e., major triad shapes, dominant seventh shapes, minor shapes, and diminished seventh shapes. With guitar music being written one octave higher than it actually sounds it makes sense that Charlie Christian would play his solos primarily on the first four strings of the guitar, first through fourth strings. On an electric guitar those notes sound very clean and clear (particularly if you use an unwound third string; some jazz players even use an unwound fourth string!). Some licks can be played in more than one shape; some work best out of one particular shape, e.g., the F chord shape is the one most used for the major triad family of chords. It is really up to the player to determine which shape or scale to use that best fits the musical phrase being played.

Each chord shape has a range of notes, particularly the notes available on the first string; that range will often determine what chord shape you might choose to play a particular lick out of. Then again, if you want to play mainly on the first and second strings for a cleaner, leaner sound your choice of shapes will necessarily change to allow for that to happen; if not, then playing out of one particular shape may work just as well.

The basic F, D and A chord shapes are formed from major scale forms. The fingering for some chord shapes may vary from that used to play the scale; sometimes they will segue into the next logical chord shape; some have "transitional" shapes, which are really subsets of a particular chord shape (e.g., the E chord shape is a subset of the F chord shape); and sometimes a different left hand finger might be used for the same note in a chord shape which will affect what scale notes can then be stopped out of that particular shape.

This book will be best understood if you can read treble clef staff notation and have a basic working knowledge of intervals, scales and chord construction.

I would like to begin by presenting the major scale, in which either the second or fourth finger is used to stop the Root of that scale on the sixth string. The popular jazz scale fingering using the index finger to stop the Root does not yield any viable triadic chord shapes on the lower bass strings; however, that shape is used for the Long *A* chord shape on the treble strings and when playing various minor scale forms, e.g., minor pentatonic, the blues scale, etc.

Let's start by playing the Bb major scale by stopping the Root, Bb, at the sixth fret on the sixth string. If we begin that scale with the second finger of the left hand you will see that all of the scale notes in the lower octave are easily found "under the fingers." Please note that this octave is played across three strings. For the upper octave, the Root begins with the little finger on the fourth string; this fingering also works naturally.

If you look at the notes of the triad (Root, third and fifth) for the upper octave you might have noticed the familiar **"F" chord shape**.

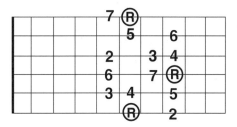

Here it is on a fingerboard diagram:

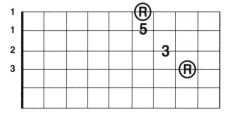

Did you also notice that the left hand fingering for the scale in the upper octave does <u>not</u> match the common fingering we often use for playing the F chord shape? This will happen for some other chord shapes as well, depending on what notes are being played within the chord shape itself.

Now, let's play the same Bb major scale but beginning with the fourth finger on the sixth string at the sixth fret, instead of the second finger.

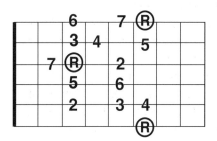

You should notice two things: (1) <u>it takes four strings to play the lower octave</u> instead of three, as when you began with the second finger and (2) one note of the scale, the leading tone or seventh major scale degree, is "out of position," i.e., you have to move your index finger down one fret to stop that note, then reposition that same finger up one fret in order to play the octave note of the scale. The stopping of those "out of position" notes [I notate such notes in my examples as *o/p*] sometime lead to an alternate usage of "transitional" chord fingerings.

What notes are deemed "out of position" can vary from one chord shape to another: sometimes it may be the sixth scale degree, sometimes the leading tone, sometimes the supertonic, etc. The fingering of the upper octave, beginning with the index finger this time on the third string, results in what is commonly called in traditional guitar circles as the **"Long A" shape**. This shape allows you to play one complete octave (Root to octave) on the top three strings.

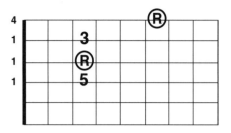

The D chord shape is formed by playing the Root of the scale, in this case D, on the fifth string at the fifth fret with the fourth finger. Because the scale is begun on the fifth string it is only possible to play one complete octave, fifth through second strings:

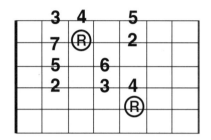

Did you notice that the triad in this shape looks a lot like the C shape in first position? We will call it the D shape since the fifth and third notes of the scale are stopped.

C Chord Shape

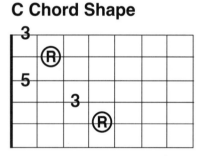

There is another *A* chord shape, in which only the notes up to the flatted seventh can be logically stopped on the first string. If you play the D scale but beginning with the second left hand finger instead of the fourth, and continue playing into the upper tetrachord of the second octave, you will notice the regular *A* **chord shape**. In order to segue into the *A* chord shape from the D chord shape you will need to change fingerboard positions by moving the third finger up one fret, from the seventh scale degree to the Root on the third string.

A Shape:

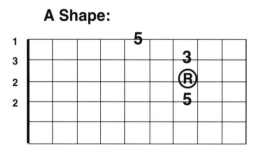

Note that the Root of both A chord shapes are located on the same fret, only the left hand finger used to stop that note is different, which results in the two different chord shape formations.

Each of these three chord shapes - F, D and A - represent a different inversion of the same triad, i.e., the repositioning of the notes in order: Root to third to fifth. An easier way to visualize this is, for instance, to remember that the Root of the F shape can be found on the first string of that shape (actually this is the octave note); for the D shape the Root moves to the second string of the D shape; and for both A shapes the Root is found on the third string: thus, by simply locating the Root of the chord on the treble strings you will automatically know which chord shape to use: F, D or A respectively.

Also take note that the notes at either end of each chord shape are identical, i.e., the low and high notes of the F

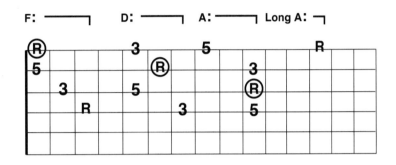

shape is the Root; of the D shape is the third; and of the regular *A* shape is the fifth. Now that you see how the F, D and A chord shapes are formed from the major scale you should practice playing complete triads [Root, third, fifth and octave] and Major Sixth chords [i.e., Root, third, fifth and sixth notes of the major scale] in each shape, beginning with the Root of the chord shape to get used to how the shape works. Try it now in the key of F by using the F chord shape at the first fret of the fingerboard (the Root is located on the fourth string at the third fret, the octave on the first string at the first fret).

Here is a "quick reference guide" to help you figure out the voicing for the Major Sixth chord inversions:

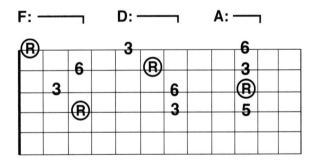

Now, let's look at a few characteristic idiomatic techniques Charlie Christian used so that you can immediately begin to incorporate them into your playing.

Glissandos. This technique involves sliding up to a note (the beginning point of the gliss is up to the performer) to begin a phrase or descending after the last note of a phrase is played. Gliss' are often notated by a short diagonal line leading to or away from a note, sometimes by a squiggly line for a longer glissando.

Cadential Endings. One of the easiest ways to begin sounding like Charlie Christian is the approach he used to end phrases. For instance, in the case of a phrase ending on the Root, he often played that note as a dotted quarter note followed by an eighth note, the third of the chord, usually sliding into that latter note by use of a gliss <u>or</u> by playing a grace note (usually the augmented second); on occasion he also reverses the procedure by using a gliss or grace note to approach the Root, then playing the following third of the chord without any alteration. Here are some examples in various guises, including some examples of phrases ending on the fifth, sixth and Major seventh which occasionally were used by Charlie Christian:

It is interesting to note that if you invert the Root-third cadential ending you end up with one of the common 1940s bebop cadences:

[be - bop]

Single Note/Chord Usage for Rhythmic Emphasis. Another interesting technique is the use of single notes or partial chords to create rhythmic emphasis for comping purposes or to end a solo phrase; Django Reinhardt often used this technique. Here are a representative number of examples of single note usage used by Charlie Christian; the use of rests to create syncopation makes these single note phrases stand out even more:

Occasionally, repeated single notes are used <u>to</u> <u>begin</u> a phrase or lick:

Mordent. This is a 3-note ornament where the first note is played, then the scale note immediately above (sometimes a half-step) is hammered on, then pulled off, creating a triplet rhythm (notated as). This ornament is often used to break up repeated quarter notes.

Django Reinhardt loved to use this technique in a variety of ways; here are a few examples as used by Charlie Christian:

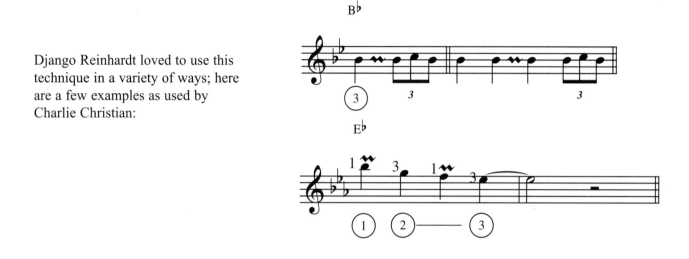

Bent Notes. The use of bent notes is a common country blues guitar technique; Django Reinhardt also used them beginning with his earliest recordings made in the mid-1930s. The target note is ordinarily approached from a <u>half</u> <u>step</u> below by bending the lower note <u>up</u> <u>to</u> the target note. The original note is then usually returned to, either by a release of the note just bent or by playing that original note with the pick. Usually, the note bent to is the one that begins a phrase or that is the highest note of a phrase.

Pedal Notes. Charlie Christian occasionally used a pedal note in his phrasing. Here is an example in the key of G major:

G pedal:

Octaves. The use of octaves is not a regular technique found in Christian's solos, as it is in Django Reinhardt's playing or even Oscar Moore's playing (Oscar's playing style at that time emulates several of Django's better known stylistic licks) in the recordings that he made in 1937-38 with the Nat King Cole Trio, a couple of years before Charlie Christian made his first recordings with Benny Goodman. Here are two typical usages that Charlie Christian used:

F

CHAPTER FOUR

CHORD SHAPES

I will primarily be using staff notation for the examples provided throughout this book, although from time to time I will use guitar tablature for purposes of clarity for certain left hand fingerings when considered appropriate. For anyone who doesn't read music you fill find that by closely comparing the staff notation and tablature to the fingerboard diagram you will find yourself reading through the examples with little effort, as most of the notes used in these single note licks are contained within the chord shape itself.

Since the examples in each section of this book ordinarily use only one particular key per chord shape this in itself will reinforce your understanding when reading through them. Once you are familiar with how a chord shape works and feel comfortable playing licks out of it you can then move that shape around the fingerboard just like Charlie Christian did: playing the licks on adjacent frets, a minor third apart, a Perfect Fourth away, etc. In other words, once you know how a lick sounds and how to play it you no longer have to really "read" that lick in staff notation; simply reposition the chord shape and play the lick.

F CHORD SHAPE. Let's begin by looking at the fingerboard diagram for the F chord shape. I have decided to use the key of Bb for this particular chord shape as it is a common jazz key and it is also positioned in the middle of the fingerboard. As you can see, the Bb scale is laid out in staff notation and guitar tablature under the diagram, including suggested left hand fingerings (including out of position notes, i.e., notes that do not fall into the "four finger per position" dictum).

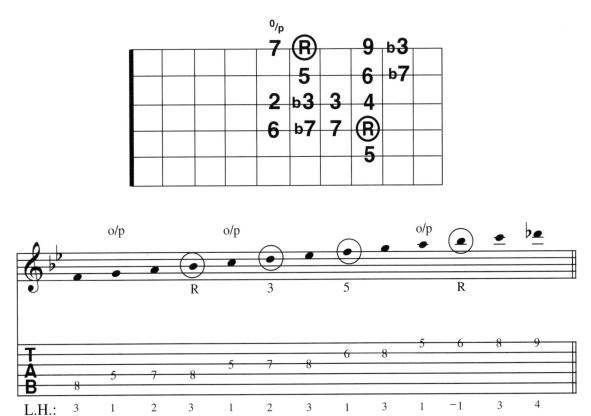

Triads. Triads are often used as pickup notes to begin or to end a phrase (e.g., the octave note will often terminate the pickup note sequence, while for a tag ending the Root is often the note which begins the concluding part of the lick). Depending on how many beats need to be filled, the rhythm of those notes may vary from eighth notes, triplets, etc., and its position within the bar, i.e., which beat, can also vary. Interestingly, Charlie Christian doesn't often use straight arpeggio rolls in his solos except for pickup note figures.

Here are some examples of triad usage used to <u>begin</u> phrases; note that the concluding octave falls on the downbeat across the bar line:

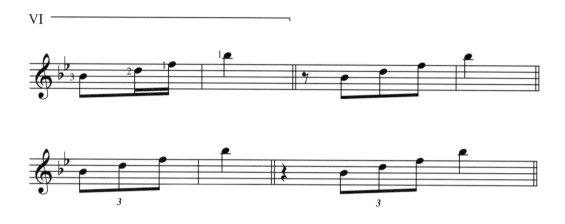

Here are some examples of triad usage used to <u>end</u> phrases. Here, the octave note does not fall on the downbeat, as that note would usually be the Root, sometimes the third or fifth:

The ninth of the chord, i.e., one octave higher than the second scale degree, is often used to lead back to the octave note of the triad (just as the supertonic often leads to the tonic). Here are some examples of that practice:

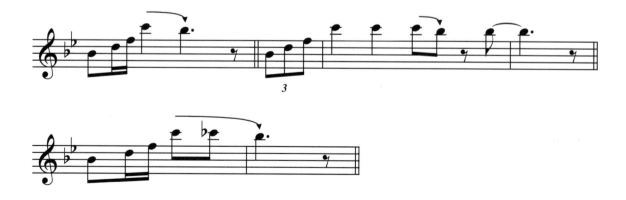

Charlie Christian often used an augmented second (+2) to lead to the third of the chord to break up the notes of the triad. Here are some examples of triads in Root position:

+2

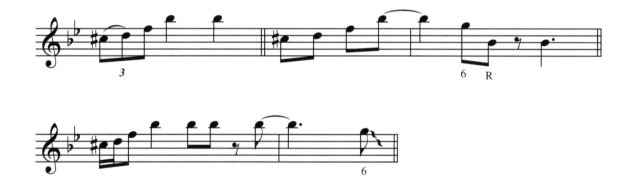

A note of caution: it is very easy to accidentally play eighth notes instead of triplets, even though triplets may be notated; however, the feel is completely different. The rhythm is often dictated by how many beats remain before the next downbeat. Of course, feel free to experiment using different rhythms; sometimes either rhythm will work in a given phrase. Charlie Christian used many different rhythms for his use of triads, so we should feel free to do likewise. The augmented second can also be used to begin triadic note sequences instead of the Root:

Licks. The licks Charlie Christian uses often have three distinct parts: (1) an introduction (i.e., pickup notes); (2) the main lick itself; and (3) a tag ending (which can vary according to how you want the lick to terminate). Sometimes the pickup notes and/or tags are such an integral part of the lick that you cannot easily separate them from the lick itself.

Charlie Christian used a wide variety of pickup notes and tag endings, which are mostly interchangeable, so you can pick and choose which sounds best to you to introduce and end a lick. In many cases, they do not really affect the sound of the lick itself.

Augmented Second - Third Scale Note Sequence. As just noted above, a lick frequently used by Charlie Christian consists of the movement of the augmented second to the third scale degree. This two-note sequence is very common in traditional country blues guitar, used in a variety of guises. As Charlie Christian played country blues guitar it is not surprising to see its use in his solos; tenor sax player Lester (Prez) Young also used it quite a bit, and Charlie Christian idolized Prez's playing.

Another reason for Charlie Christian's using it with greater frequency in the F chord shape is the fact that the second note of the major scale is out of position, while the augmented second is not: no doubt Charlie Christian felt that it was probably just simpler to substitute the augmented second instead of moving his left hand all of the time to stop the supertonic.

We can conclude this because when you look at other chord shapes he often uses the major second scale degree with regularity when it is part of the chord shape itself. When looking at the major scale, the fourth scale degree can often be seen as resolving, or falling back, to the third, a half step away (similar to the supertonic-tonic motion discussed earlier). An embellishment Charlie Christian often used was to interject the augmented second in between these two scale degrees. This 3-note figure could be looked at as a chromatic approach note figure, the fourth descending to the target note of the third via the augmented second (this half-step above, then below, the target note is a common bebop surrounding tone enclosure technique).

Make note that most of the time when using this particular note sequence the concluding third resolves to the fifth of the chord (but not always!) and that the positioning of the note sequence relative to the downbeat will vary. As the augmented second is enharmonic with the flat third blue note it creates a tension between minor and major tonalities. Music theory dictates that you can only have a chromatic flat third scale degree when descending (unless it is part of the diatonic scale/key signature); ascending you should use the enharmonic spelling of the augmented second. Also, the augmented second always resolves upward when it acts as a chromatic passing tone.

I have also included an example of a standard four-three bebop enclosure for comparison; note the off-beat position of the fourth scale degree.

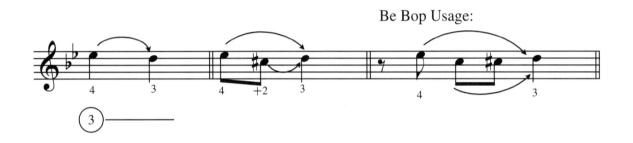

Be Bop Usage:

TetraFragments. In playing many of the licks used by Charlie Christian out of the F chord shape it became clear that he was using a handful of mini-licks, or licks-within-a-lick. I am going to call these mini-licks "*tetrafragments*." Since a tetrachord is a four-note sequence, i.e., the first four notes of a scale (called the lower tetrachord) and the last four notes of the scale (called the upper tetrachord), and since the "core" licks Charlie Christian uses usually consist of four or five notes I have coined the term *TetraFragments*, as those notes are usually based on either side of a targeted chord tone. Without question, the core *tetrafragment* of the F chord shape lick is based around the fifth note of the scale:

T/F Evolution:

Track 1

Track 2   T/F

Note the delayed rhythm of the *tetrafragment* in this example:

Here are some variations on this *tetrafragment* using the octave and sixth scale degrees <u>to</u> <u>lead</u> to the fifth of the chord. Note that these particular phrases end on the Root, fifth, or octave:

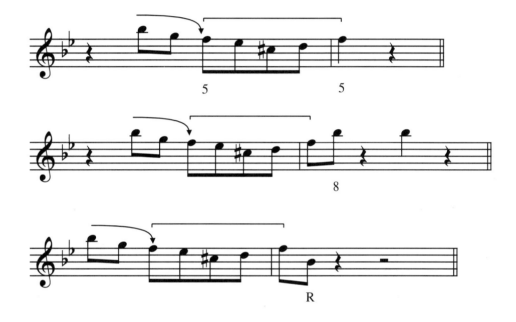

Here are a couple of additional examples using different pickup note configurations:

Track 3

Track 4

Next are a few examples where the augmented second is used as a passing <u>grace note</u> within the core *tetrafragment*:

Track 5

Here is an interesting, longer example using the fourth scale degree twice in succession creating the necessity for a triplet rhythm in order to successfully complete the *tetrafragment* phrase:

Track 6

Next is an example using the sixth <u>below</u> the Root, an out-of-position note; also note the Charlie Christian Root-to-third cadential figure to conclude the phrase:

For purposes of comparison, let's look at a common F chord shape lick used by Django Reinhardt; in this particular example Django <u>does</u> <u>not</u> <u>use</u> the fourth scale degree:

16

The sixth-flatted sixth (6-b6) scale note sequence is often used to lead to the core *tetrafragment*, as it is easily playable within the F chord shape. Here is an example:

Track 7

The octave note often appears <u>before</u> the sixth-flatted sixth (6-b6) note sequence. In the following examples the octave note is positioned on the weak beat; the eighth note rest on the downbeat creates a certain degree of forward motion in the phrases:

Track 8

The next two examples position the octave note <u>on</u> the downbeat:

Track 9

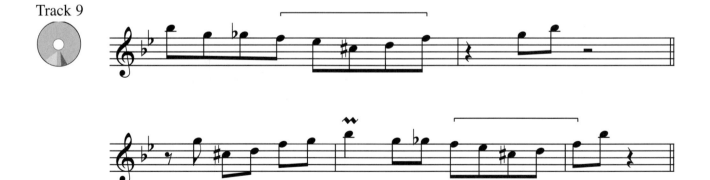

Here are a few examples using the ninth scale degree as part of the pickup phrase to add some tonal color:

Track 10

Track 11

Next, let's look at some commonly used phrases examples using the flatted seventh (b7) scale degree in the *tetrafragment*. Note that the flatted seventh moves to the sixth scale degree then the fifth, thus the flat sixth is not used here. In this case you could say that the flatted seventh-sixth note sequence is a substitute for the sixth-flat sixth note sequence (b7-6 vs. 6-b6) as both sets of notes resolve to the fifth. The last two examples in this set do not use the fourth scale degree.

Track 12

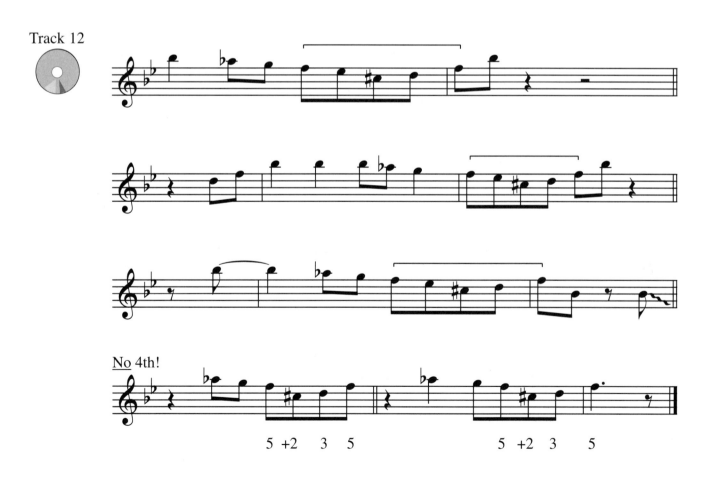

Here are a couple of examples where the *tetrafragment* does <u>not</u> resolve on the fifth scale degree; also, note the use of a long glissando used to begin the phrase on Bb in the second example:

Next is a slightly longer phrase using a "blues"-like introduction; you could repeat the phrase, ending on the Root instead of the fifth:

Track 13

Here is an example where the augmented second-third note sequence is used twice: once as a grace note, later on as a sixteenth note:

Track 14

The fourth-augmented second-third note sequence can also be used to begin phrases. Here are some examples:

Here is a longer example where the core *tetrafragment* is used, followed by the fourth-augmented second-third note sequence to end the phrase:

Next is an unusual example using three consecutive sets of triplets, including the use of the out-of-position sixth scale degree to conclude the last triplet figure:

Let's now look at the augmented second when it is used to <u>begin a phrase</u>. First are some examples in a pentatonic scale situation:

Next are two phrases, which include the use of the flatted seventh:

Here is an example where the augmented second-third note sequence resolves to the Root instead of the fifth. Does this phrase sound familiar? It should, as it is the basis for the chorus of the song, *St. Louis Blues*:

The augmented second-third note sequence can also be used to begin a riff:

21

Next are a number of examples you could consider using as tag endings:

Here is an example using the flatted ninth (b9) and flatted sixth (b6) as chromatic passing tones on the weak beat:

Track 15

b9   b6

To close out this section on the F chord shape I am presenting a number of examples of "blues" licks commonly used by Charlie Christian:

E CHORD SHAPE. The E chord shape is what I call a transition chord created by the necessity to play the sixth scale degree <u>below</u> the Root [i.e., the submediant], another out-of-position note in the standard F chord shape. Basically, it is simply a variation of the F chord shape: think of capoing the first position F chord shape at the first fret, then observing that the remaining two-note stopped shape is an E chord shape; add the fifth below the Root and you will easily see the familiar looking first position 3-note E chord shape on the fifth, fourth and third strings. For this section I am going to use guitar tablature as it's meaning is clearer in intent, rather than marking up each staff notation example with position, string and fingering markings.

Here is the basic core *tetrafragment* of the E chord shape:

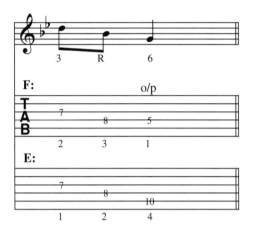

As you can see, in order to play the sixth scale degree in Bb using the F chord shape you have to move down one fingerboard position and play that note with the index finger; to play the sixth scale degree in the E chord position you must make a fingering change on the third of the chord by stopping it with the index finger instead of the second finger, thus in the E chord shape the sixth scale degree is now stopped by the fourth finger on the fifth string at the tenth fret.

Here is a diagram of the guitar fingerboard showing these two alternate fingering schemes

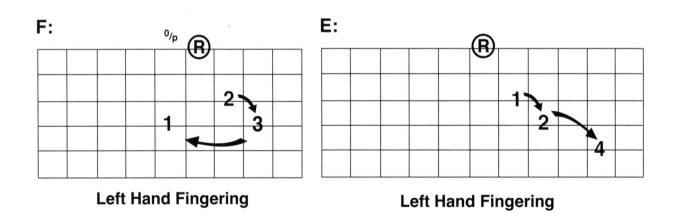

F: **E:**

Left Hand Fingering   **Left Hand Fingering**

Now, let's now look at an example using this core *tetrafragment*:

As you can see, I provided <u>four</u> different left hand fingerings in tablature for this one phrase:

(1) the first fingering scheme is typical, playing the sixth scale degree on the fourth string with the index finger then returning to the F chord shape;

(2) the second fingering is played entirely out of the E chord shape, no fingerboard shifting is required;

(3) in the third fingering I begin the phrase in the E chord shape but make a return to the F chord shape, as sometimes the phrase will continue out of the home chord shape, e.g., for a tag ending; and

(4) I actually change chord shapes from F to the Long A chord shape by using a different left hand fingering to stop the sixth scale degree on the fourth string.

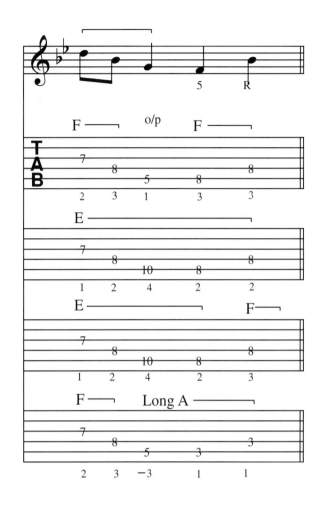

Next is an example similar to the one just looked at except that is uses the leading tone to return to the Root, instead of the fifth as in the previous example:

Track 16

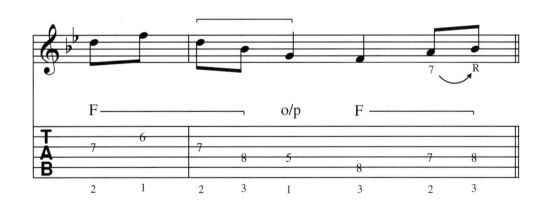

Here is the same example using a pickup note sequence (no tab provided). Note that you could play this phrase entirely out of the E chord shape using the left hand's fourth and second fingers to stop the pickup notes.

Here is a slightly more intricate passage:

In the first tab the entire example is played out of the F chord shape except for the out-of-position sixth scale degree; in the second tab it is played entirely out of the E chord shape. This is one of the interesting things about using this chord shape. I think that by now you are beginning to see the logic of how and why to use the E chord shape.

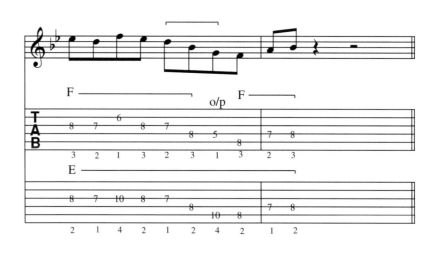

When the augmented second-third note sequence is used, the augmented second often acts as the pivot note to change chord shapes. As previously shown, the augmented second is often fingered by the index finger, so that finger is the one used to move up one fret to the third of the chord to change fingerboard positions as well.

Here is a basic example using the F chord shape, then using the pivot fingering to transition into the E chord shape:

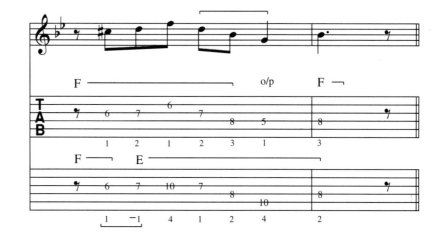

Next is a slightly longer variation on the above example:

Track 17

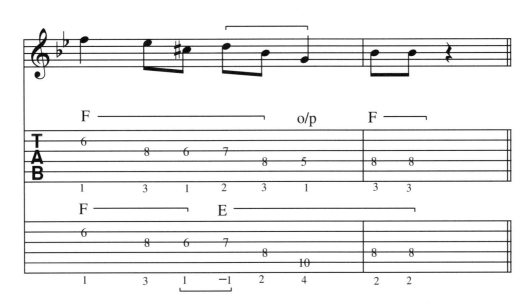

Gibson Guitar demo in early 1940
for New York band Instrument Co.

Here are a couple of examples of the augmented second positioned on the weak beat to begin the phrase:

Track 18

28

In the next example the augmented second begins on the downbeat. This particular phrase ends with a Charlie Christian cadential figure; add a gliss to the Root or the third as you see fit to emulate his usual cadential sound.

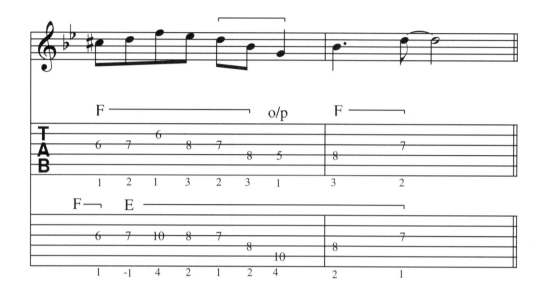

Now, for a slightly more complicated example I will leave the fingering up to you to figure out.

Early 40's

Here is an example of the use of the augmented fourth (enharmonic with the flatted fifth), following the sixth scale degree, used as a chromatic approach note to the fifth of the chord:

Track 19

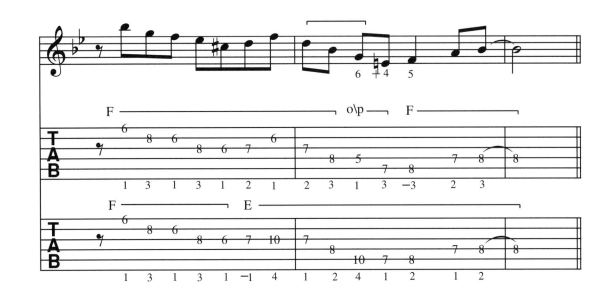

Next is an example of the sixth-flatted sixth (6-b6) passing tone note sequence that we used earlier to kick off the F chord shape core *tetrafragment*. Watch the rhythm of the delayed final note of the phrase and ending gliss!

Track 20

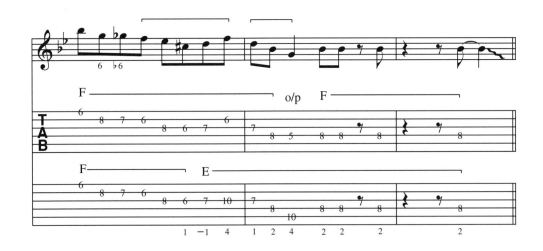

Here is a relatively innocent looking phrase using the flatted second scale degree as an accented passing tone. In the F chord shape this phrase is quite awkward to finger due to the out-of-position second scale degree; using either the E or Long *A* chord shape you will find that it is much easier to execute.

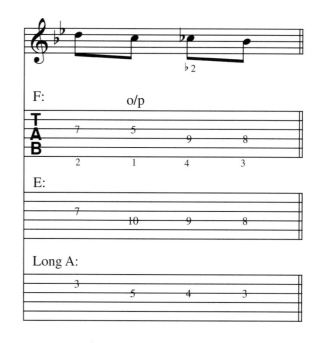

Here is an example of how Charlie Christian uses this note sequence to end a phrase:

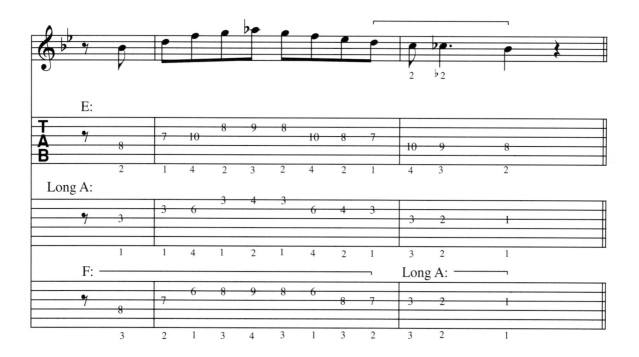

Let's move on the D chord shape.

D CHORD SHAPE. For this chord shape I will be using the key of F as, once again, it keeps the chord shape in the middle of the fingerboard (as Bb did for the F chord shape). Below is a fingerboard diagram and F scale in staff notation and guitar tablature:

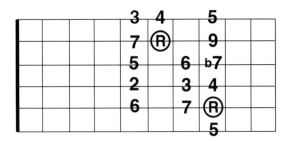

D Chord Shape

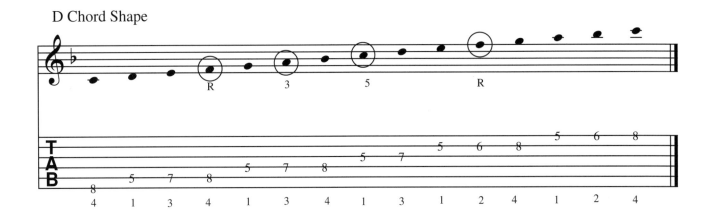

Unlike the F chord shape, the usual pickup notes for the D chord shape are invariably those of the chord shape itself on the top three strings: the fifth, Root and third. In order to create a sense of forward motion an eight note rest is usually positioned on the downbeat followed by the pickup notes, perhaps even a triplet figure.

Track 21

The sixth scale degree <u>below</u> the Root is located holistically within the chord shape and is often used, creating a minor chord shape based on the sixth scale degree. Since I am using the key of F for the D chord shapes, this minor chord would be D minor. However, it does not function as a minor chord; in fact it is related to the F major sixth chord.

Track 22

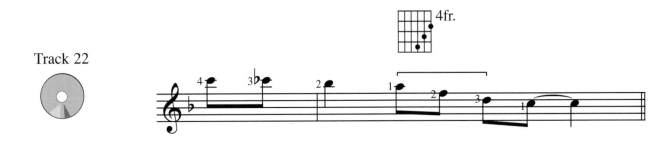

The basic *tetrafragment* of the D chord shape includes the use of the chromatic flatted fifth (b5) passing tone: 5-**b5**-4-3. Here are a number of examples (keeping in mind that any pickup notes Charlie Christian uses are more-or-less interchangeable). Note the out-of-position augmented second note on the first string in the last example below [there is also an augmented second on the fourth string in the D chord shape; however, it is positioned within the shape itself]. I will provide some additional examples of this usage on the first string later on in this section.

Track 23

Track 24

A variation on the basic *tetrafragment* is use of the flat sixth (b6) scale degree as a passing tone:

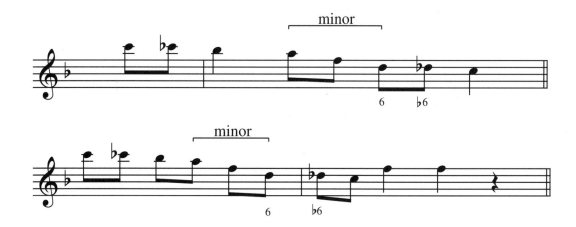

33

In the D chord shape, the sixth-flatted sixth (6-b6) note sequence can also be used to lead to the core F chord shape *tetrafragment.* Here are a couple of examples:

Track 25

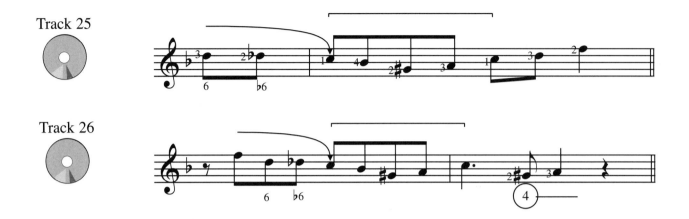

Track 26

The augmented second-third note sequence is used fairly frequently in the D chord shape. Here are two similar examples:

Next are two examples in a pentatonic scale note sequence:

Here is an example where the target note is the flatted seventh:

In the next example note the use of the flatted fifth (b5) <u>and</u> flatted sixth (b6) chromatic passing notes:

The augmented second-third note sequence positioned on the first string is also often used, as demonstrated in the following examples; note the metrical positioning of the augmented second on the weak beat:

Track 27

Track 28

The use of the augmented second can make a phrase sparkle. Compare the following two phrases: which do you prefer?

THE REGULAR *A* CHORD SHAPE. As I mentioned in Chapter 2 when discussing the formation of chord shapes from major scales, there are two shapes for using the *A* chord. For right now, we are going to use the Regular A chord shape.

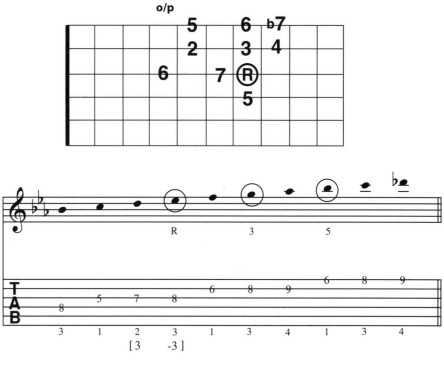

I am using the key of Eb as the reference key here, as once again it is positioned in the middle of the guitar fingerboard. Several differences to keep in mind between the regular *A* chord shape and the Long *A* chord shape are the range of notes on the first string; the way the dominant seventh chord is formed for each of these shapes; and that the sixth scale degree below the Root is not part of the regular *A* chord shape (thus out of position) but *is* part of the Long *A* chord shape.

While there is no one particular *tetrafragment* used in the regular *A* chord shape there are some interesting licks that Charlie Christian played out of it.

The first is a way to approach a Major Sixth chord:

The next example is a common cadential figure:

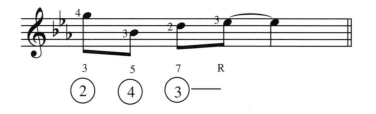

The next phrase targets the fifth of the chord. Note that the last four notes constitute the common digital fingering pattern, 1-2-3-5 (the first four notes of the pentatonic scale); in this case the "1" does not begin on the beat, resulting with the fifth arriving on the downbeat:

Track 29

The augmented second-third note sequence is also used in the Regular A chord shape. Here is an example most of you will be familiar, having hear it countless times in many different song genres:

The fourth-augmented second-third note sequence is also used in this chord shape. Here is an example in which the lick is used to target the Root:

The fifth can replace the fourth, as shown in this three-note sequence:

Track 30

The augmented second can also be used as a chromatic approach note to the third scale degree:

Here are some examples of the augmented second-third note sequence used to begin phrases in the Regular A chord shape:

Track 31

There is one note in the Regular *A* chord shape which is "out of position" and that one is the sixth scale degree below the Root. Here are three examples:

Track 32

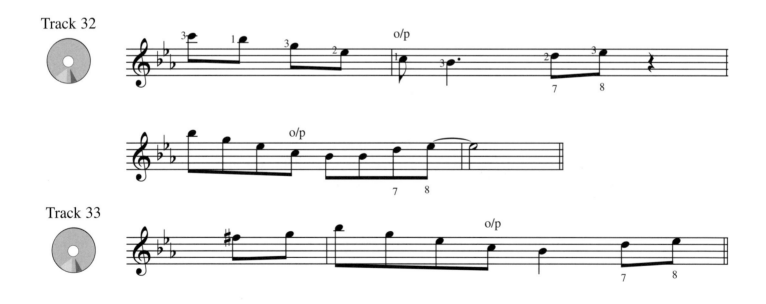

Track 33

To end this section I would like to provide a few "blues" licks that work well out of this chord shape:

THE LONG *A* CHORD SHAPE. Below is the fingerboard diagram and scale/tab for the Long *A* chord shape:

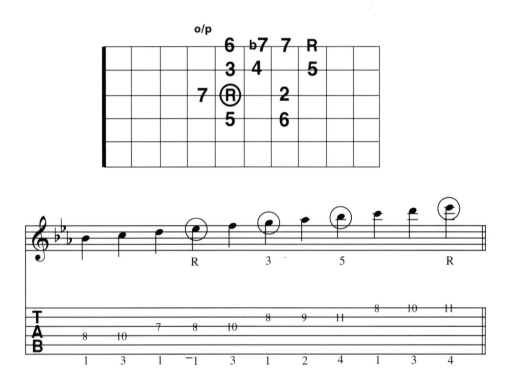

It is quite easy to play the pentatonic scale in the long *A* chord shape. Here are two examples:

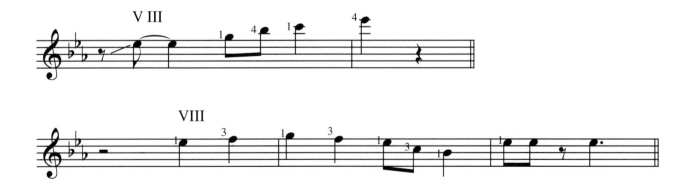

Next is an upper tetrachord note sequence whose notes fit more naturally, for instance, in the F chord shape than in the Long *A* chord shape:

Long A Shape: D Chord Shape:

Here is a similar example using the fourth and sixth scale degrees:

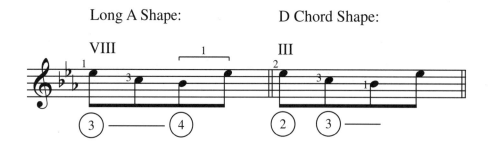

The Major Sixth chord is easily formed from this chord shape by barring the first four strings.
Here are a few examples of that usage:

Here are four similar examples targeting the Root:

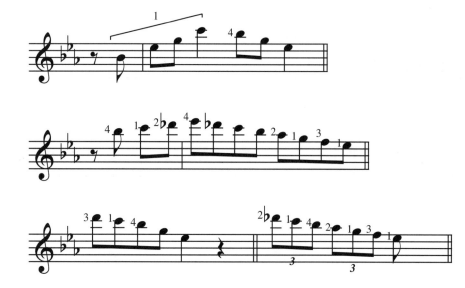

Next are some examples using the sixth-flatted sixth (6-b6) note sequence:

In the following example please note the use of the out-of-position augmented second on the first string used to begin the phrase:

Charlie Christian also used the flatted fifth (b5) note in the Long *A* chord shape. In the second of the following two examples note that I have **not** used enharmonic spellings for the augmented fourth and flatted fifth but have used the "politically correct" music theory spellings. The augmented fourth is used in the ascending phrase, while its enharmonic equivalent, the flatted fifth, is used in the descending part of the phrase (note the arrows pointing this out):

Here are four examples using the supertonic and flatted second scale degree note (2-b2) sequence (or nine-flat nine [9-b9] note sequence, if you prefer to think of it that way):

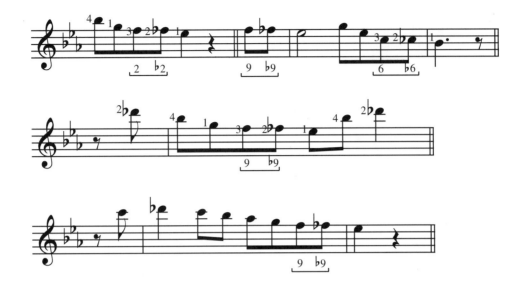

Next are some examples using out-of-position notes in the Long *A* chord shape, i.e., the augmented second <u>and</u> the leading tone:

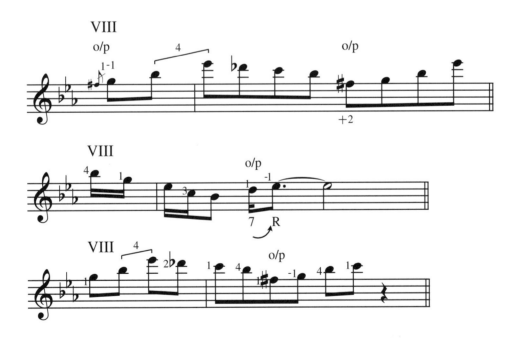

Let's move on the dominant seventh chord shapes.

CHAPTER FIVE

DOMINANT SEVENTH CHORD SHAPES

THE F7 CHORD SHAPE. Let's begin our survey of dominant seventh chord shapes by looking at the F7 chord shape. I will be using the key of B flat for these examples.

First, let's look at the chord shapes for F and F7:

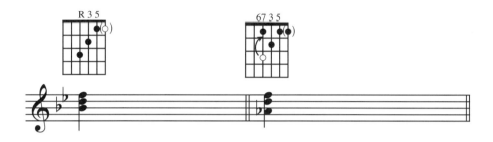

As you can see, the only difference is that the flatted seventh of the chord is played on the fourth string instead of the Root. These lowest three notes — the flat seventh, third and fifth — are often used to begin a phrase using this chord shape.

Here are two examples where this chord shape targets the sixth scale degree (or thirteenth):

September 22, 1940 with Harlan Leonard's Kansas City Rockets at Lincoln Hall in Kansas City. Left to right front Fred Beckett, Charlie Christian, Henry Bridges and Effergee Ware.

When used as pickup notes, the rhythm of this chord shape can vary from eighth notes to triplets to beginning on the weak beat. Note the inclusion of the flatted seventh (b7) in the following examples:

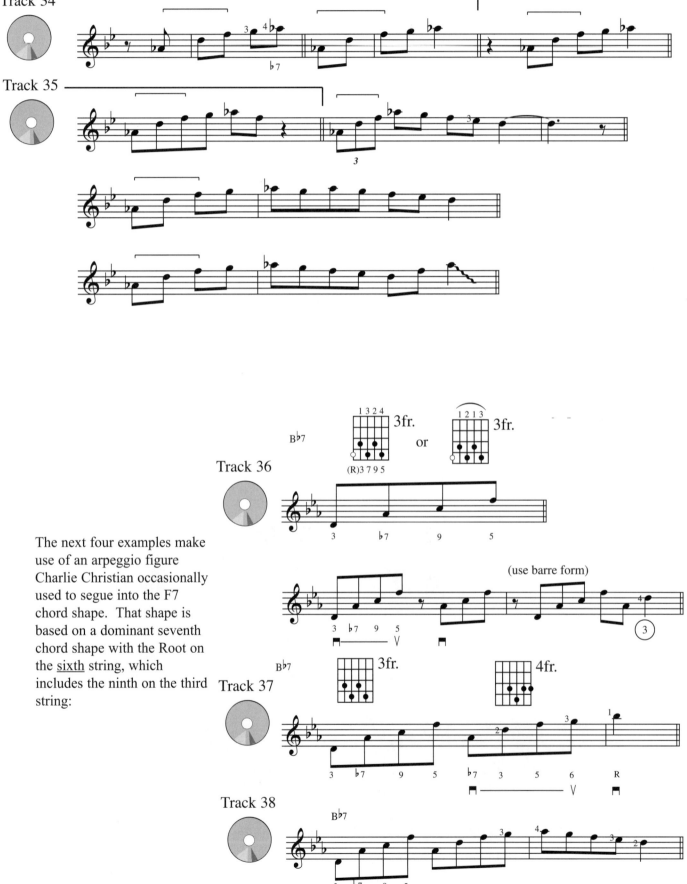

The next four examples make use of an arpeggio figure Charlie Christian occasionally used to segue into the F7 chord shape. That shape is based on a dominant seventh chord shape with the Root on the <u>sixth</u> string, which includes the ninth on the third string:

Let's expand the range of the use of the F7 chord shape to include the octave and/or ninth scale degrees:

Track 39

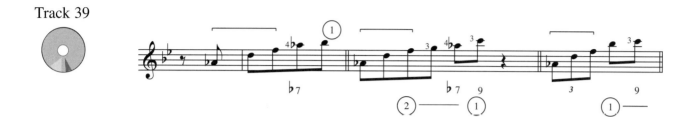

This next example is interesting is that it includes a passing flatted ninth (b9) chromatic approach note used to connect the F7 and the Long *A* chord shapes:

Track 40

Here is an example using the descending 5-3-2-1 digital pattern. While you could play this phrase out of the F chord shape, an interesting thing to note is that the fingering I use here resolves to an E7 chord shape (which is a subset of the E chord shape), including the out-of-position note second scale degree, which, as you know, is not in the F chord shape. Having said that, the phrase could have just as easily segued into the Long A7 chord shape. All three possibilities are outlined below:

Track 41   Track 42

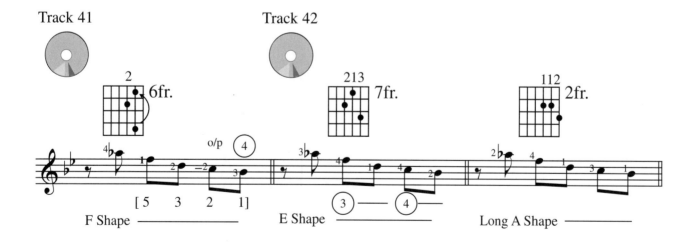

F Shape   E Shape   Long A Shape

In the next examples I have added an E7 chord shape to end the phrase for emphasis:

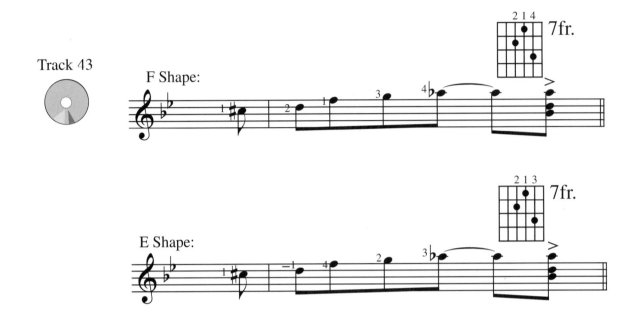

Track 43

The following example begins with a chromatic line in Bb using the E chord shape, then shifting into the F7 chord shape, first as a passing chord (B7 in this case) then to the targeted Bb7 chord; also included is an almost identical phrase using sixteenth notes instead of eighth notes:

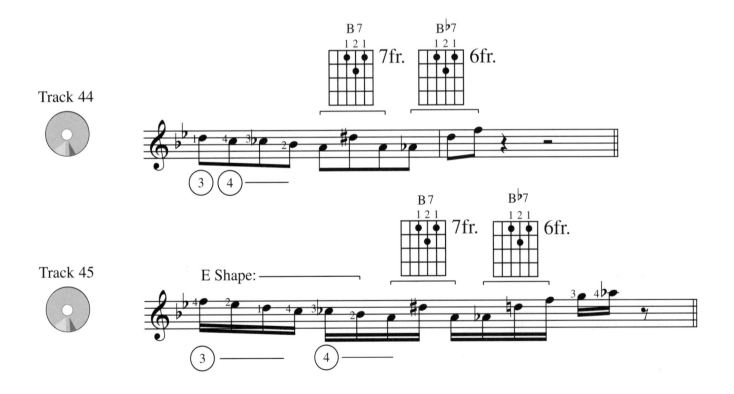

Track 44

Track 45

Next is an example ending with a descending arpeggio figure where the last few notes form the F7 chord shape. Although you could play these notes using the standard chord shape fingering it might be more prudent to consider playing the phrase using a different left hand fingering <u>within</u> the chord shape. Also, watch those two beginning triplets!

Track 46

Obviously, if the lower flatted seventh is <u>not used</u> you can play blues licks out of either the F or F7 chord shapes. Here are two typical examples:

Track 47

That concludes the F7 chord shape. It is basically used as a set of pickup notes to begin a phrase.

Benny Goodman Sextet 7 November 1940. Left to right: Georgie Auld, Benny Goodman, Cootie Williams and Charlie Christian.

THE D7 CHORD SHAPE. There are two things that need to be kept in mind as we go through the D7 chord shape examples: the first is that although this shape should be a simple subset of the D chord shape, i.e., playing the flatted seventh below the Root on the second string, the left hand fingerings are different than you might expect. Why? In comparing the two chord blocks below you will see that (1) the Root for the D shape is on the <u>fifth</u> string, while in the D7 chord shape the root is on the <u>fourth</u> string, thus a different set of fingerings needs to be used, and (2) a minor chord based on the fifth of the V7 chord is often an essential element of the phrases. As I will be using the key of F for the D7 chord shape examples, the minor chord will be C minor using the A minor chord shape. Another feature of the D7 chord shape is the somewhat more frequent use of chromatic passing tones: 2 to flat 2, 3 to flat 3, etc.

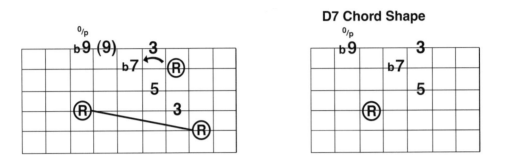

Let's begin by looking at the basic *tetrafragment* of the D7 chord shape, the minor chord shape. It begins on the third of the F7 chord, which in this chord shape happens to be out-of-position, and frequently ends on the upper third. Here it is:

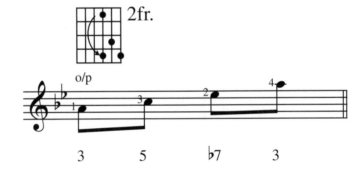

Next is an example of the *tetrafragment* using a slightly different rhythmic scheme ending with a tag that includes the seven to flatted seventh (7-b7) passing tone:

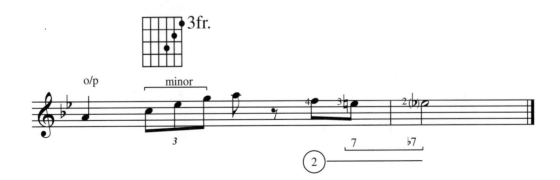

48

Let's now focus on descending forms of the *tetrafragment*. Here is a very basic xample followed by a phrase using the same notes but, as per my past practice, showing an altered rhythmic scheme:

Track 48

The following example, ending on the flatted seventh, could be used a pickup phrase for the basic *tetrafragment*:

The next two nearly similar examples target the Root, using a descending 5-3-2-1 digital pattern:

Track 49

The following examples use a flat nine to nine (9-b9) note sequence at the beginning of the phrase. Note that the flatted ninth and lower third are both out-of-position notes here. Once you shift to the lowered third (A) you could consider completing the phrase out of the E chord shape:

Track 50   Track 51

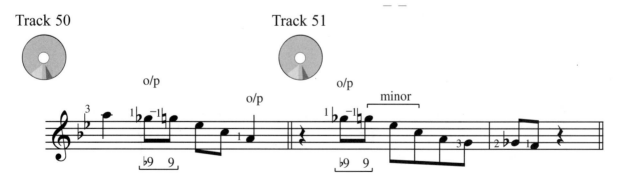

49

The next two examples both begin on the upper third of the F7 chord and use a two to flat two (2-b2) note sequence, one octave lower than the nine to flat nine examples just shown. Once again, the lower third (A) is the out-of-position note in the phrase:

Here are two phrases using a third to flat third (3-b3) note sequence (the second example also includes a second to flatted second (2-b2) note sequence as well). Notice how easily they both integrate into the core *tetrafragment*:

Track 52

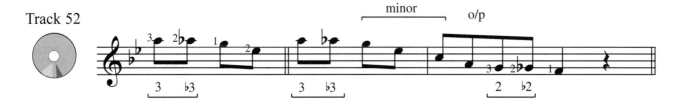

Next are a couple of examples that do not happen to use the minor chord shape; note how the second scale degree segues into the E shape:

Track 54

Track 53

Here is a more complicated phrase using the fifth-flatted fifth (5-b5), third-flatted third (3-b3), and the second-flatted second (2-b2) passing tones, as well as a minor chord shape. Quite busy!

Track 55

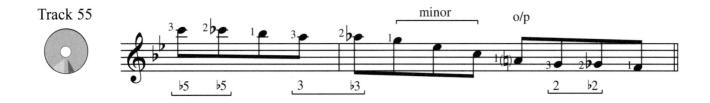

50

Now, let's look at phrases using contrary motion, i.e., descending motion followed by ascending motion. Here are four examples demonstrating this usage:

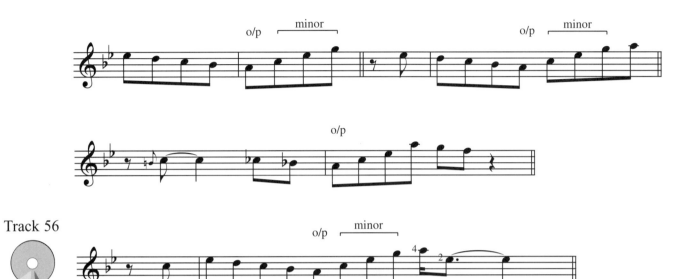

Track 56

Charlie Christian, Benny Goodman and Harold Covey
at the Waldorf Astoria, New York, late September 1939.

Next are a number of examples where an ascending arpeggio is used to end the phrase. Again, note that some of these examples are quite similar except for the position within the beat where the phrase begins.

Track 57

The next phrase uses two chord shapes, the D7 followed by the F7 chord shape:

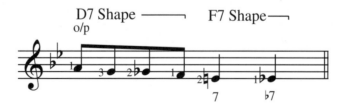

The following two examples begin with the F7 chord shape but end with the D7 chord shape:

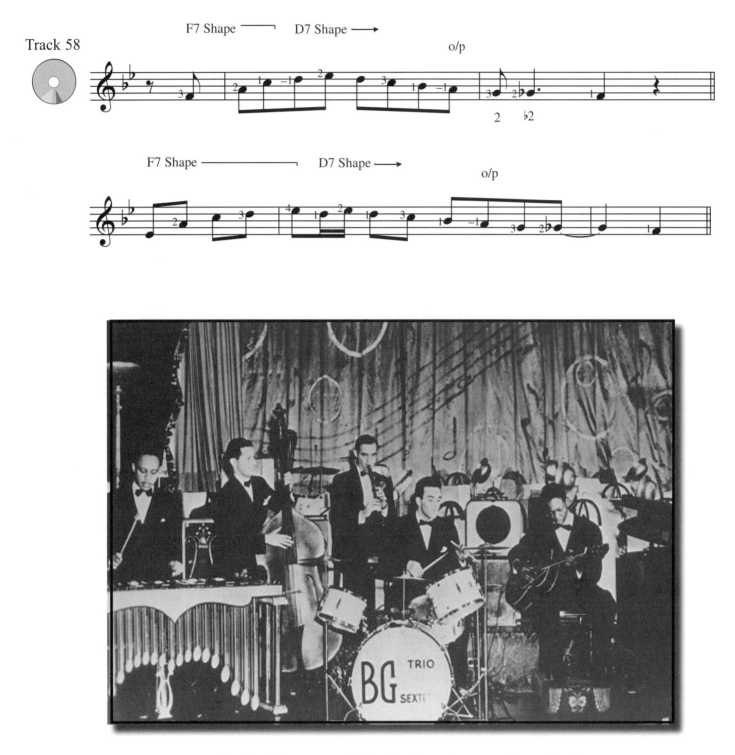

Charlie Christian with the Goodman Sextet at the Waldorf
Astoria Hotel December 1939

The following examples use shifting chord shapes (D7 chord shape to the F7 chord shape); note the passing F7 chord shape outlined. Earlier we looked at a similar example using this technique.

Track 59

Finally, here are a couple of usages using the notes contained within the chord shape itself:

THE OPEN A7 CHORD SHAPE. This particular chord shape is quite intriguing as it is often used to form the second half of a dominant ninth or thirteenth chord shape (V9/V13) whose Root is on the fifth string, so the common note sequences in this particular chord often contain the extension notes of the basic V7 chord: the 9th, 11th and 13th.

The open A7 chord shape, based on the regular A chord shape (I will be using Eb7 as the basic dominant seventh chord in the following examples), also features the use of vertical fingerings by the index and ring fingers, mostly notes from the pentatonic major scale, including what is the ninth of the V9 chord. To slightly complicate matters, many of the phrases we are going to look at can often be played by using the F minor chord shape (i.e., as noted earlier, the second inversion of the dominant seventh chord is a minor chord), thus the choice of using three different but related left hand fingerings! While this will initially be confusing, in the end it will result in greater flexibility in your ability to play these types of phrases.

Let's begin by looking at the V7 and V9/V13 chord shapes and how they are interrelated. The following diagram shows visually that the shape of the Eb7 chord is the same as the lowest three notes of the C7 chord in first position, the Root relocated to the sixth fret (a minor third higher than C) on the fifth string; the second finger is used to stop the Root instead of the ring finger, as in the first position C7 chord:

C7:

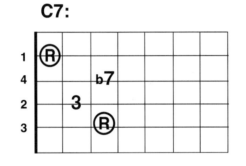

The next diagram shows the standard open A7 chord shape on the top four strings of the guitar with the flatted seventh located at the sixth fret on the third string (thus, the Root is located at the eighth fret). It is important to keep in mind that you do not have to maintain these chord shapes in order to effectively play out of them, e.g., you can use the third, first and fourth fingers to stop the lowest three notes of this chord shape as the note positioned on the first string is not always necessary to stop. It is helpful to think of it as a 3-string chord shape, somewhat like the F7 chord shape on the fourth, third and second strings.

Eb7: Open A7 Chord Shape

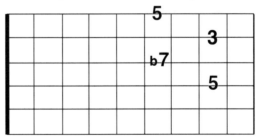

Next is an example of an open A7 chord shape using the F minor chord shape at the sixth fret; the necessity of stopping the fifth of the chord on the first string is the reason why this chord shape appears visually the way it does.

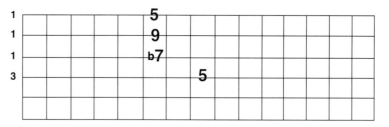

F minor Chord Shape

A change of fingerboard position is easily made by shifting the left hand fingering of the basic V7 shape on the flatted seventh of the chord, i.e., from the third finger to the index finger on the third string (similar to the pivot note used in the E chord shape). If you were just going to play the notes within the chord shape of the V9 or V13 alone then I suggest maintaining the fingering of the chord shape; however, if you are going to introduce passing tones within the chord fingering, other than perhaps a flatted thirteenth, then I strongly suggest that you switch fingerboard positions to take advantage of the fluidity of using the index and ring fingers vs. the second and fourth fingers to stop those passing notes. Also, if you want to stop the higher flatted seventh below the octave on the first string then you will need to be playing out of the open A7/F minor chord shape, as the thirteenth is the highest note available in the standard V13 chord shape.

Please make note of the fact that the third of the V9/V13 chord is found in its chord shape but not in the open A7 chord shape, where it is an out-of-position note on the fourth string. Of course, if you decide to work out of the open A7 or F minor chord shapes when playing V9/V13 chords then the third of the chord will also be out-of-position. As the Root of the V9/V13 chord is often not even played, those phrases invariably begin on the third of the chord. In fact, in analyzing Charlie Christian's solos it seems clear that when the third appears as the lowest note it often indicates that the V9/13 chord shape will be used. The Root of the V9 chord is occasionally used, but ordinarily as part of a descending line targeting that note.

I know that what I have just laid out is a quite confusing to digest, so let's begin by looking at some common note sequences found in the open A7 chord shape, then go on from there.

Here is an example in the open A7 chord shape using an ascending mixolydian (V7) scale pattern, beginning on the third of the chord. As the notes are stopped on first two strings there is no need for any type of barre as the ninth on the second string is not stopped; you could also use a glissando to approach the third.

The next two examples demonstrate the use of the ninth and/or the augmented second as a passing tone to the third or as a grace note and/or a chromatic passing tone. Again, a barre is not required to play these particular phrases:

Track 60

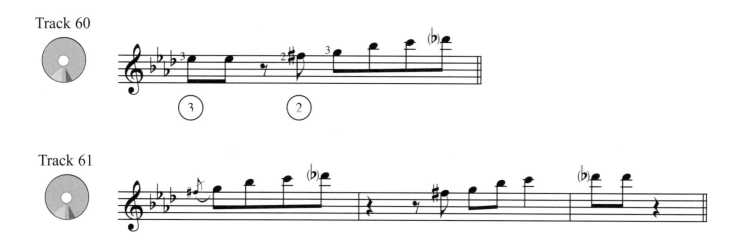

Track 61

The next example is a longer phrase where you could use either the open A7 chord shape or the F minor chord shape. In this case, using a barre is more efficient to use, as the lowest note is the flatted seventh on the third string. Also, make note of the Major Seven to flatted seventh (7-b7) passing tone.

Track 62

The open A7 chord shape has several distinctive *tetrafragments*. The first is a descending scale from the third descending to the flatted seventh; I have included two additional examples of its usage:

57

The next *tetrafragment* involves the scale degree sequence 5-9-3-b7-R-9. The fifth is often used as a pivot note to end the pickup note phrase as well as to begin a particular *tetrafragment*. In this example, the third and the Root are approached by the ninth and flatted seventh respectively, thus targeting the chord tones positioned on the beat.

Here are three examples using this particular *tetrafragment*. I have placed brackets over the note sequences:

Track 63

Benny Goodman and His Sextet at the Paramount Theatre, New York, 16 April 1941. Left to right: Georgie Auld, Benny Goodman, Charlie Christian, Artie Bernstein and Cootie Williams.

Now, let's use the F minor chord shape. The following examples use the Bb (fifth below the Root), stopped by the ring finger, and the ninth, so it is often more economical to use a barre (experiment alternating between a three- or four-string barre) as it is less stressful than moving the index finger back and forth across the strings. Also, most of these examples use the out-of-position third of the chord on the fourth string as the concluding note of the phrases.

Track 64

Track 65

Track 66

59

Two of the next three examples target the Root of the V9 chord:

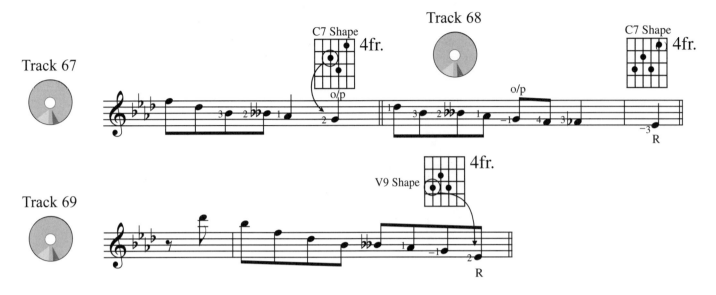

Track 67

Track 68

Track 69

It is now time to look at another *tetrafragment*, 3-5-b7-3-9. Note that a barre, working out of the F minor chord shape, is often useful when playing this particular *tetrafragment*:

Here are four examples of this usage. Once again, I have bracketed the *tetrafragment* note sequences for you.

Before we move on to the V9 and V13 chord shapes proper, here are a few final examples using a combination of two of the *tetrafragments* I have just presented, as well as some out-of-position note usage.

THE V9 AND V13 CHORD SHAPES. The following diagram shows the standard V9 and V13 chord shapes:

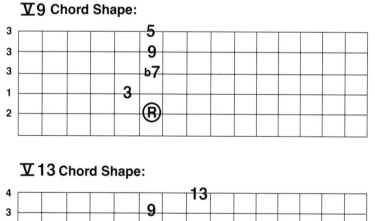

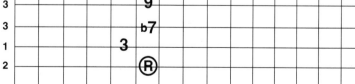

Here is an example using the standard V9 chord shape. Note that this shape doesn't make use the Root on the fifth string, as shown in the previous chord diagram:

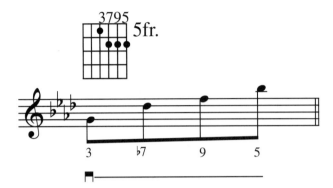

The following two examples, which are identical except for the rhythms involved, use the fifth as the lowest note instead of the third and also use the thirteenth to target the fifth. As a result, it is better to use the F minor chord shape here and the fourth finger to stop the thirteenth.

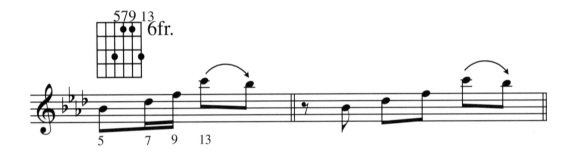

The next example outlines the classic rootless V13 chord shape, which doesn't include the fifth, since it is positioned on the same string as the thirteenth:

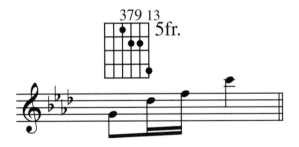

The following phrase demonstrates the use of the F minor and V13 chord shapes; note the triplet rhythm usage used to end the phrase:

Let's now look at the V13 chord, but with the introduction of the fifth stopped within the chord shape itself on the fourth string (not the first string this time!). Once again, note that the note sequences are essentially the same.

Here are a few similar examples using the thirteenth to approach the fifth, touched on earlier; the use of the F minor chord shape is more effective here. Again, note the changes in rhythm for the same note sequence; I have pointed this out numerous times as it demonstrates Charlie Christian's flexibility in his use of the same harmonic material by shifting it on different beats in the measure(s) and/or with different rhythms.

Here are some examples for you to experiment in using the V9, F minor or open A7 chord shapes, or a combination of them. While it is possible to play all of these examples using the V9 shape, you may find that the hand is less stressed in using the other two chord shapes. Also, note the use of the flatted thirteenth in the last example of this set:

In the following example the thirteenth resolves to the ninth, instead of the fifth as in past examples:

Here is an example where the V9 chord shape is used to good effect in the first half of the phrase, while the open A7 chord shape is more effective in the second half :

In this final example the V9 chord shape is a better choice due to the out-of-position third scale degree for the execution of the triplet rhythm and concluding notes rather than using the F minor chord shape:

Let's move on the minor chord shapes.

Photo Top Left: *The Benny Goodman Sextet at the New York World's Fair in September 1939. Left to right: Charlie Christian, Benny Goodman, and Nick Fatool.*

Photo Top Right: *The Benny Goodman Sextet at the Waldorf Astoria, New York in December 1939. Left to right: Johnny Guarnieri, Charlie Christian, Artie Bernstein, Lionel Hampton, Nick Fatool and Benny Goodman.*

Photo Center Right: *Benny Goodman's band in a recording session with Charlie Christian, Lester Young, Buck Clayton, Count Basie, Freddie Green, Walter Page and Jo Jones.*

Photo Bottom Right: *Benny Goodman Sextet November 1940. Left to Right: Bernie Leighton, Charlie Christian, Cootie Williams, Georgie Auld, Benny Goodman, Artie Berstein and Harry Jaegar.*

THE F MINOR CHORD SHAPE is simply a modification of the F chord shape (and, obviously, of sound quality). In the following examples I will be using the key of B flat minor; the lowered third scale degree (Db) will be positioned on the third string at the sixth fret resulting in a familiar barre shape, as its use was discussed in some detail in the last chapter regarding the open A7 chord shape.

Here are a number of examples using the basic F minor chord shape:

Track 71

Track 72

Next are a couple of examples using a descending note sequence; note the use of the mordent in the second example:

Here are three examples of phrases played on the top two strings only:

Track 73

Track 74

Track 75

The following example uses the out-of-position second scale degree on the third string:

The next example uses a common usage for outlining minor chords, the 1-3-4-5 digital pattern:

[1   3   4   5]

Charlie Christian with the Count Basie Orchestra at the Apollo in October in 1940. Left to Right: Count Basie, Charlie Christian, Walter Page, Benny Goodman, Jo Jones, Earl Warren and Buck Clayton

The following phrases all end on the tonic note. In the first example note the use of Charlie Christian's favorite cadential lick but, naturally, using the minor third instead of the major third to end the phrase.

Track 76

Track 77

Track 78

These two examples use the leading tone, A natural (thus, use of the melodic minor scale):

Track 79

Track 80

THE D MINOR CHORD SHAPE.
Interestingly enough, Charlie Christian's solos do not often seem to accommodate the D minor chord shape fingering. The reason for this seems to be that an entire change of fingering is required from the standard D chord shape to the D minor chord shape. Let's compare the two shapes to see why:

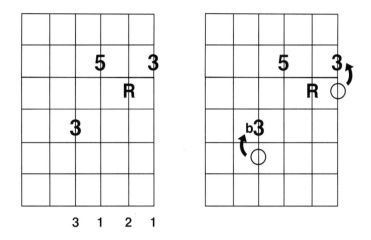

You can see that you have to deconstruct the 3-string barre and rearrange the left hand fingers to go from the major to the minor shape; even though you can keep the third finger on the fourth string to act as a guide finger you still have to change fingerboard positions, so it is not a seamless transition as in the F minor chord shape.

When the D minor chord shape does fit in, it is usually for the notes contained within the shape itself. Here are two examples in the key of F minor; note the out of position lower Root in the second example:

THE A MINOR CHORD SHAPE. The A minor chord shape is easily formed by lowering the third of the regular *A* chord shape; the examples below will all be in the key of D minor. Incidentally, there is no minor chord shape for the long *A* chord, as the minor third and fifth can only be stopped on the second string.

As usual, let's look at some examples of the notes contained in the shape itself:

Now, let's look at some examples where the second scale degree is used as a passing tone in the triad:

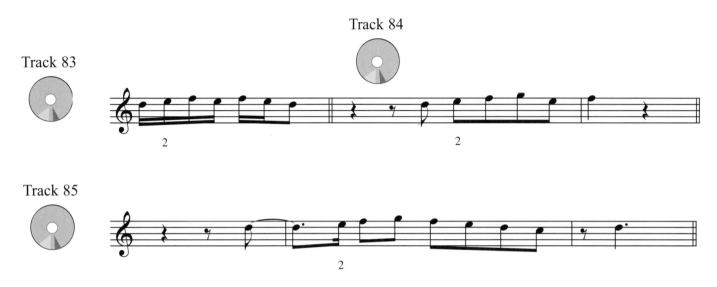

Track 83

Track 84

Track 85

Here are some related phrases based on the Root-second-third scale degree note sequence, leading to a riff:

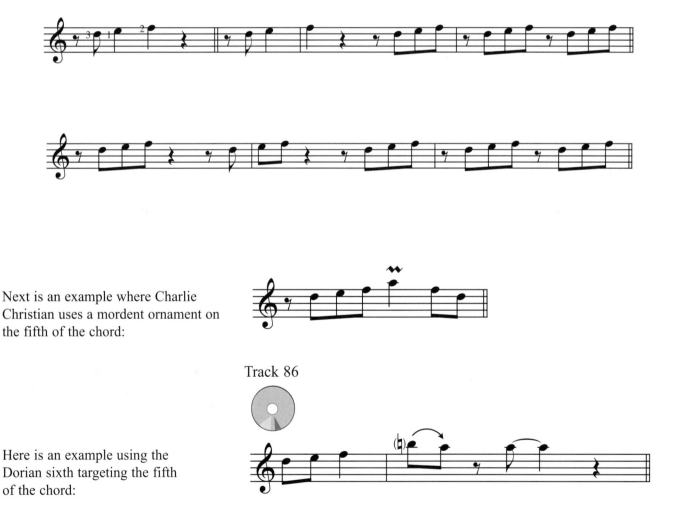

Next is an example where Charlie Christian uses a mordent ornament on the fifth of the chord:

Track 86

Here is an example using the Dorian sixth targeting the fifth of the chord:

The Dorian sixth below the Root is an out-of-position note in the A minor chord shape. Here are a number of examples demonstrating that usage:

Track 87

Track 88

Track 89

The chromatic augmented fourth is also an out-of-position note on the first string. Here is one example:

Track 90

Here are some examples where the phrase ends on either the fifth or the Root out of the triad:

Track 91

Track 92

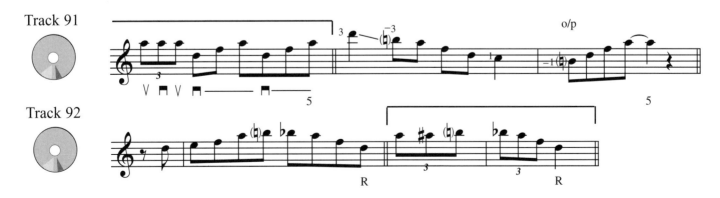

71

While there is no clear *tetrafragment* in the A minor chord shape, the following note sequence of the Dorian sixth leading to the triad is close to one. Of course, as noted above, the Dorian sixth is one of the standard out-of-position notes in this chord shape. In the first example, once again note the use of a mordent on the fifth of the chord; the second example basically consists of the notes of the pseudo-*tetrafragment*; the final example is a longer phrase where an entire measure or so is played out-of-position.

Finally, here are a few concluding examples for you to examine. The first is a riff beginning on the third scale degree (note the passing tone on the second scale degree); the second example consists of a descending/ascending minor seventh chord ending on the ninth; the final example uses a V-I cadence, the V chord being an A minor chord in this example.

Track 93

CHAPTER SEVEN

THE DIMINISHED [°7] TRIAD

This triad consists of notes with intervals of a step-and-a-half apart between them, e.g., B-D-F. The usual function of this chord is to connect two chords or inversions of a chord, although it can be part of the voicing of another chord, e.g., a first inversion dominant seventh chord.

Due to the symmetrical intervallic nature of this chord there are various ways that the notes can be connected on the fingerboard. The following diagram, using three string shapes (thus, one inversion of the chord will be missing), covers many of those possibilities:

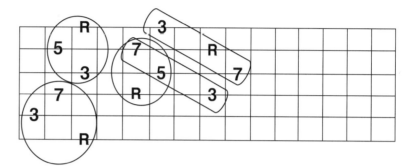

Since this book primarily concerns chord shapes on the top four strings of the guitar, the shape for the diminished chord used in common practice is:

You may have noticed that in this chord shape, while all of the notes of the diminished chord are present, they are not in their correct alphabetic order. The chord shape order is Root, flat fifth, double flatted seventh [sixth] and the flat third instead of Root, flatted third, flatted fifth, then double flatted seventh. Also note that there are two 3-string chord shapes contained in the overall shape: the D chord shape on the bass side and the D7 chord shape on the treble side.

One common way of using the chord shape is to strum it as a chord in one position or by moving the chord shape up or down the fingerboard; you could also apreggiate the chord, then shift. The following diagram shows one inversion of these three shapes:

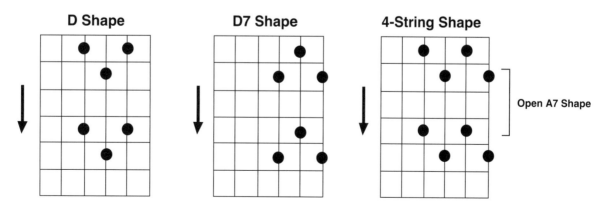

D Shape   **D7 Shape**   **4-String Shape**

Open A7 Shape

Using the G diminished triad as an example the notes from Root position would be G - B flat - D flat, thus a flat third and flat fifth above the Root; if the seventh is added then that note would be F double flat (which is enharmonic with the sixth degree of the chord, so it is not unusual to see the sixth written instead in order to avoid an excess of chromatic symbols; I will use both types of notation in the following examples). It is also fairly common practice to sharp the Root of the tonic major chord, i.e., from G natural to G sharp in this case (i.e., G#-B-D), resulting in a #I°7 diminished chord; another common practice is to play a rootless V7(b9) chord.

The following chord blocks compare the G triad and the G# diminished triad chord shapes, the third and fifth of the triad remain intact while the Root and octave move up one fret/one-half step:

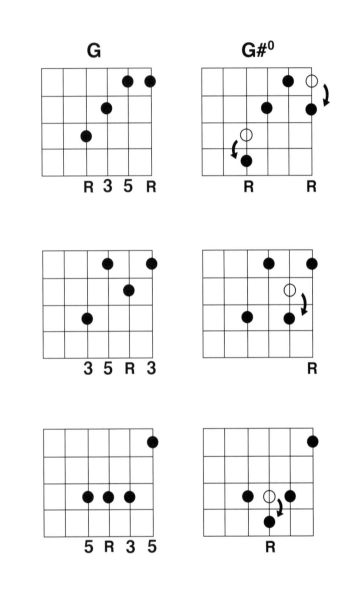

Summer 1940- Kansas City

74

I have included a number of diagrams below outlining various routings of the complete diminished seventh chord:

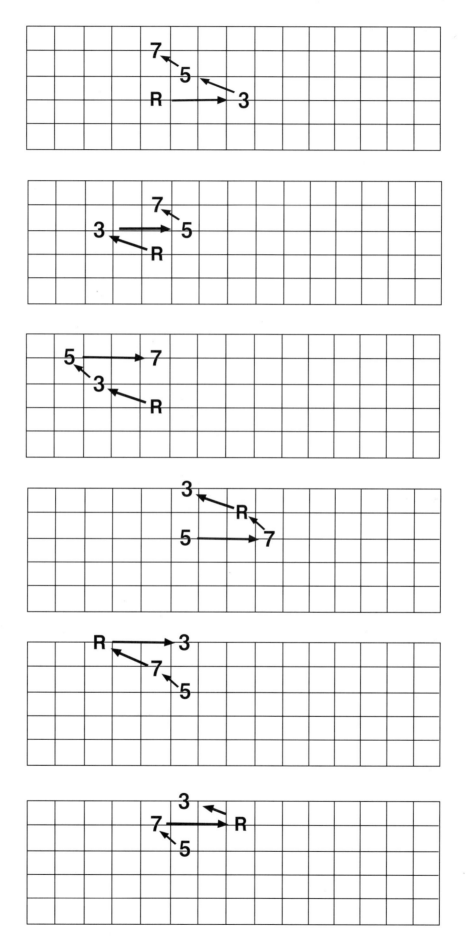

You will find that most of the following examples can easily be played out of either of the following two chord blocks, where the index finger is positioned on the lowest note of the pattern (the 1-3-4 pattern or the 1-2-4 pattern, which has one out-of-position note on the first string):

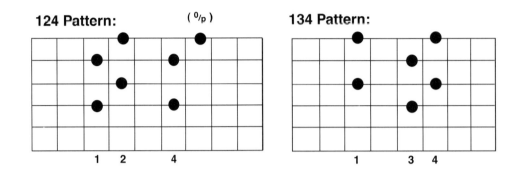

Now that we have covered the theory of how to maneuver through the basic diminished chord shapes let's look at some single measure examples as played by Charlie Christian. He often plays all of the notes of the diminished seventh chord meaning that you will have to stop one additional note in a 3-string chord shape. I occasionally mark these stopped notes with an "x" in the chord blocks when I use them; in that way you can see the basic chord shape being used.

Let's begin by looking at an example where the notes of the 3-string D chord subset shape are used; note the passing tone F sharp on beat two:

Next is a very similar example except that a stopped note is introduced after the initial note in the D pattern:

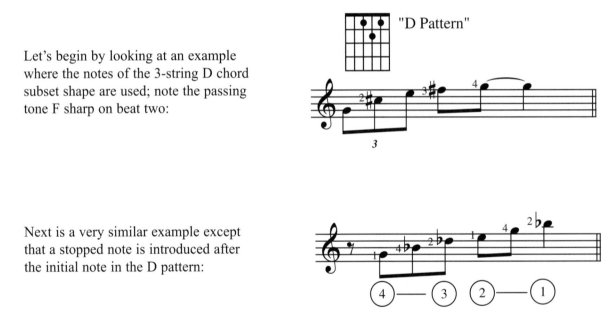

Here are two examples using only the top three strings; in the second of these please note the chromatic approach note to the E natural, as well as the eighth note rest on the downbeat:

The following example nicely shows how either 4-string diminished chord block will work:

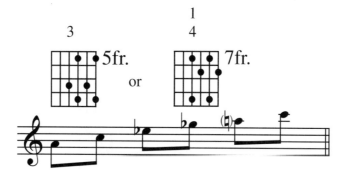

Here are a few examples of a descending diminished chord using similar fingerings:

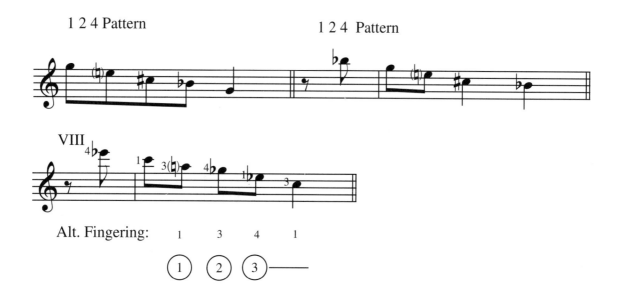

The next two examples, working out of the "D7 shape," are essentially the same except that one example begins on the downbeat, the second example doesn't:

The next example works easily out of the 1-3-4 diminished chord pattern. Note the choice of where to stop the non-position note:

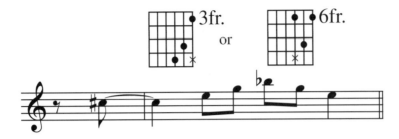

Here are two examples moving chromatically downward by half-step, essentially the same except that one begins on the weak beat while the other begins on the downbeat (note the different spelling I have used for the enharmonic notes). You could consider using the "D7 subset shape" so that you can hold the first note of the chord as an aural point of harmonic reference while you play the remaining notes of the chord shape.

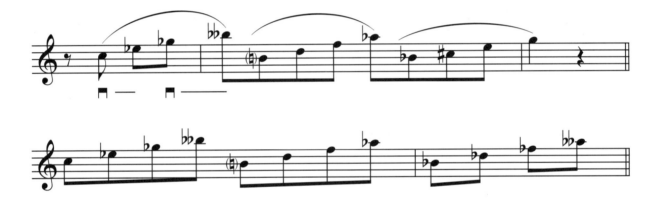

Benny Goodman Sextet, Novemner 1940. Left to right:
Charlie Christian, Cootie Williams, George Auld and
Benny Goodman.

For the final example I have also used enharmonic spellings; note the Charlie Christian cadential note phrasing. I have also provided an alternate version primarily using the first two strings:

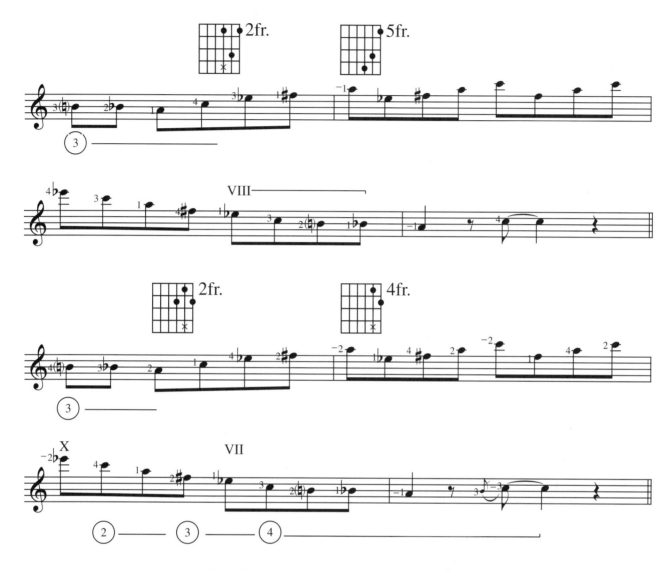

Columbia Studios recording session, New York October 1940.
Left to Right: Yank Porter, Charlie Christian,
Billy Taylor and Teddy Wilson

CHAPTER EIGHT

VERTICAL FINGERINGS

Charlie Christian occasionally used what I call vertical fingerings, which might be considered a riff or lick generally utilizing the sequential fingering across the fingerboard regardless of the chord structure underlying that movement.

As a frame of reference, here is an early example (1934) from the playing of Django Reinhardt:

Chromatic passing tones can resemble vertical fingering patterns. Here are three examples:

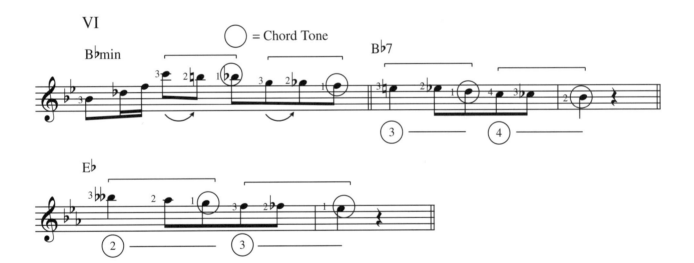

Chromatic notes <u>approaching</u> chord tones can also resemble vertical fingering patterns:

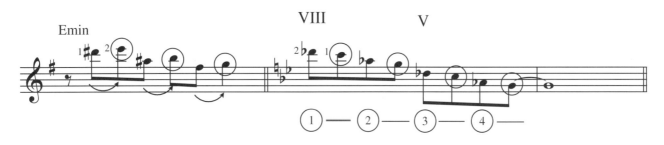

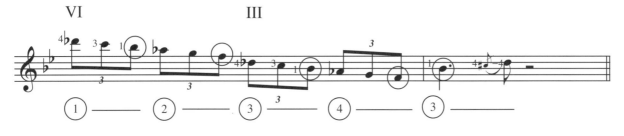

Charlie Christian at Ruby's grill September 1940. With Glenn Sam Hughes,
Dick Wilson and Leslie Sheffield.

The following vertical fingering schemes involve two fingers:

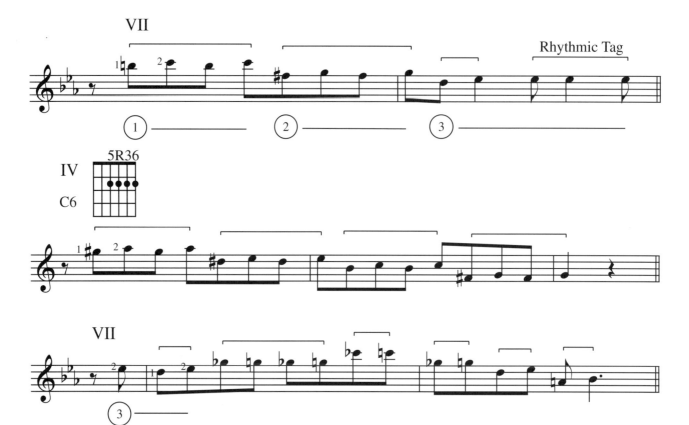

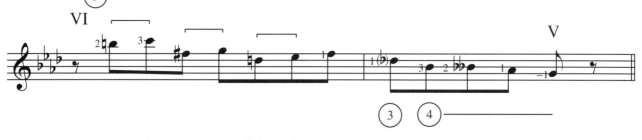

Charlie Christian with Harlan Leonard's Kansas City
Rockets at Lincoln Hall, Kansas City on 22 September 1940

The final two examples are a little unusual. The first one uses the pattern 1-2 ascending and 2-1 descending, crossing strings; the second uses a descending 3-note pattern followed by an open string, which occasionally uses an enharmonic spelling:

Summer 1940- Kansas City

Charlie Christian, particularly when playing an F chord shape on the tonic chord, would often slip in a few beats of the iv-minor chord. This is easily done as the iv-minor chord uses the same shape as the Root, third and fifth of the F chord shape. If you move that shape over one set of strings the Root is now on the third string and that chord becomes a minor chord based on the IV minor chord (using the A minor chord shape due to the change in tuning of the second string). Here is a diagram in chord block form:

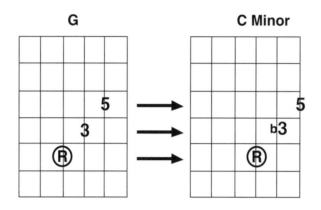

These two following examples are similar except for the rhythm. You will note that the sixth scale degree is used, thus out-of-position in this minor chord shape; you could quite easily incorporate the E chord shape fingering scheme here.

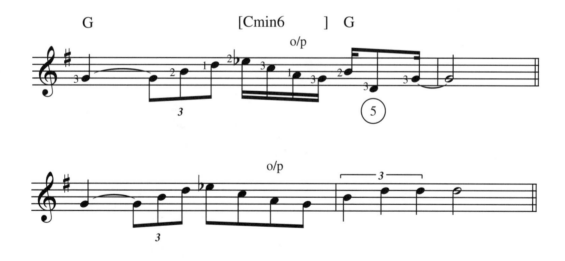

Here are two examples beginning on the ninth of the tonic chord:

It is also possible to play the four-minor chord out of the E chord shape by simply moving the three-string chord shape up one fret. Here is an example in guitar tablature:

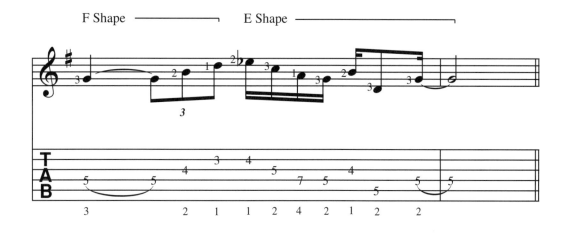

Next are several examples in the key of Bb (thus, the iv minor chord is E flat minor) where the minor triad is rhythmically altered each time that it appears. Once again, the out-of-position sixth scale degree is used, as well as the classic *tetrafragment* of the F chord shape in the last example:

The final example is one of my favorites. The Bb triad is played followed immediately by an ascending /descending E flat minor sixth chord, then ending the phrase using, once again, the out-of-position sixth scale degree to return to the tonic triad.

Charlie Christian with Benny Goodman

CHAPTER TEN

ROOT MOVEMENT
CHORD SHAPE

Now, I would like to briefly outline one procedure for choosing which chord shape to play out of. Let's use the standard 12-bar blues progression beginning in Bb. The three chords used in this progression would be Bb(7), Eb(7) [the IV chord] and F(7) [the dominant V chord]. Here is the root movement in staff notation:

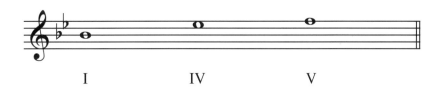

Let's look at these Root movements on a fingerboard diagram:

As you can see, the root of the IV chord is on the same fret as the Root of the tonic chord except that it is on the third string instead of the fourth string (remember, the guitar is tuned primarily in fourths). Two choices are available for the IV chord: the regular A shape (although you could use a long A chord shape here) or the D chord shape with the Root on the second string. Which shape you choose would depend on the range of notes you might want to play (also, some note sequences are smoother in certain chord shapes than in others) or you might want to try and keep the melody on the first two unwound strings for a cleaner, brighter sound. For the V chord the simplest thing to do is move up two frets from the IV chord Root or you could once again switch between chord shapes.

I Chord , Root Position

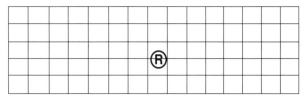

IV Chord (2 Choices)

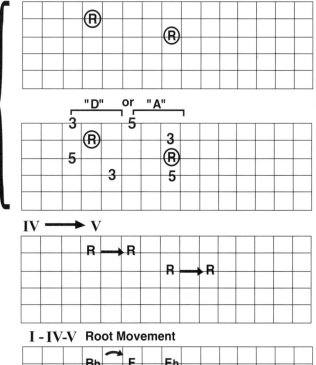

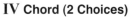

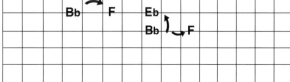

Here is a fingerboard diagram for you to refer to as a quick reference guide showing the various chord shapes on all six strings of the guitar beginning with the long A chord shape in the key of A flat:

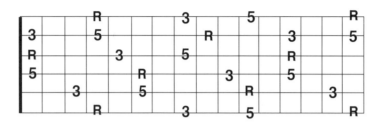

Practice going from one chord shape to another, via the melodic line, scale form or chord tone usage, deciding which note in the shape you might consider using to make the transition to the next higher or lower chord shape. Several examples presented in this book have made such chord shape changes, so look closely at how Charlie Christian does this. You will eventually find yourself subconsciously moving from shape to shape vs. playing everything out of one chord shape. This process can be compared to someone who always rides his/her bicycle in only one gear instead of using all of the available gears to maintain the same efficient pedaling cadence regardless of whether you are riding on the flats or going up- or downhill. Once you "shift gears," (i.e., change chord shapes) you will find that the fingerboard will open up for you.

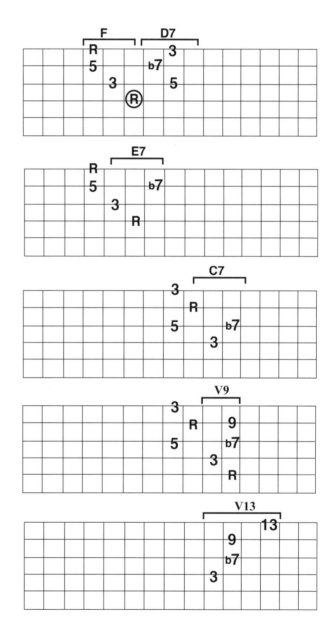

CHAPTER ELEVEN

MY PERSONAL PERSPECTIVE ON CHARLIE CHRISTIAN'S PLAYING STYLE

While there are several excellent books of transcriptions of Charlie Christian's guitar solos in today's market place it is surprising that there is so little written about his actual physical playing style. The most often published remarks regarding his guitar technique revolve around verbatim statements made by the late jazz guitarist Barney Kessel, as he was able to jam with Charlie Christian for a few days. Basically, Mr. Kessel observed that Charlie Christian used a fairly heavy guitar pick (fairly standard at that time), played mostly down strokes, and didn't use the left hand little finger too much.

While this information lays a foundation on how one might begin to approach playing Charlie Christian's guitar solos, those remarks take on much more meaning if we observe the photographic evidence of him playing the guitar, also taking into consideration his personal history of playing country blues guitar, mentioned in passing in Peter Broadbent's famous biography. As there is no known existing film footage of Charlie Christian playing the guitar, all that we have left to study are the many photographs of him playing the guitar in various situations over several years. Fortunately, much can be learned with careful observation of these photos and a basic working knowledge of country blues guitar technique, keeping in mind that the majority of the photographs consistently all show the same approach in how he holds and plays the guitar.

An often-reproduced photograph of Charlie Christian is one showing him wearing his tuxedo on the bandstand during a break, clearly playing a finger-style blues. The following things can be deduced from that one photo alone (not to mention most of the others taken of him while he is performing) as his playing style is based on traditional country blues guitar techniques:

Charlie Christian playing "fingerstyle blues" using the thumb and forefinger of his right hand on his Gibson ES150 at the Waldorf Astoria, New York, September 1939.

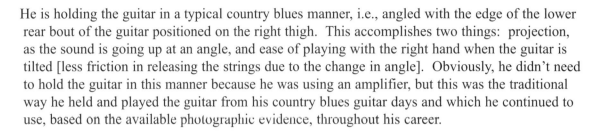

He is holding the guitar in a typical country blues manner, i.e., angled with the edge of the lower rear bout of the guitar positioned on the right thigh. This accomplishes two things: projection, as the sound is going up at an angle, and ease of playing with the right hand when the guitar is tilted [less friction in releasing the strings due to the change in angle]. Obviously, he didn't need to hold the guitar in this manner because he was using an amplifier, but this was the traditional way he held and played the guitar from his country blues guitar days and which he continued to use, based on the available photographic evidence, throughout his career.

He is using the earliest blues right hand technique: thumb and index finger (e.g., the famous blues guitarist Reverend Gary Davis also only used these two fingers to play). Christian's right hand middle, ring and little fingers are positioned on the pickguard, also typical of many country blues players, in order to steady the right hand over the strings.

The guitar neck is being held at the base of the palm between the thumb and index finger (usually referred to as "the fork" in traditional country guitar music circles) resulting in the tip of the left hand thumb being positioned at the top of the bass side of the fingerboard adjacent to the sixth string; this is also typical of old-time country guitar and country blues players allowing the player to use the thumb to stop a note on the 6th string or to dampen the open sixth and/or fifth string(s) (gypsy jazz guitarists also use this technique). This playing position also brings the left hand palm at the knuckle line directly under the base of the fingerboard, which, in turn, places the left hand fingers directly over the fingerboard for ease of stopping notes and efficient movement, i.e., less space between the fingertips and the fingerboard. While this technique would not, for instance, be acceptable in classic guitar technique, in jazz guitar technique it easily contributes focusing the movement of the left hand fingers on the top four strings of the guitar.

Charlie Christian playing what may have been Floyd Smith's Vega guitar and amplifier at the Golden Gate Ballroom in New York. Also pictured is Jack Teagarden

How did the use of country blues guitar idiomatic techniques contribute to Charlie Christian's facility playing the electric jazz guitar?Utilizing this manner of holding the guitar actually leads, for instance, to fluency in the use of down strokes; ease of playing chord shapes on the top four strings (from which his solos were developed); the use of slurs; and the use of glide strokes through the strings (lowest to highest). Glide strokes are much easier to execute when the guitar is tilted rather than vertical (where there is more string resistance), thus ease of playing through efficient movement. These strokes also provide a bigger, stronger smoother sound even when the guitar is amplified due to the pick angle when it releases the string. Also, the out-of-position sixth scale degree in the F chord shape is much easier to stop and return to shape in this guitar position than when the guitar body is positioned parallel to the chest.

Charlie Christian with his Gibson ES 150 at the First Metronone All Stars session with drummer Gene Krupa, Febuary 7, 1940

It can also be seen from the many photos of Charlie Christian that when he is playing notes on the first string his right hand middle, ring and little fingers are usually positioned on the edge of the pickguard; he rarely moves them past the half-way point on the pickguard when playing on the lower strings, even the fifth and sixth strings (there is also a photo of him using a pick to play notes on the fifth or sixth string). The point is that those three fingers are always <u>on</u> the pickguard, just like a country blues guitarist finger's are always positioned on the pickguard of an acoustic guitar.

There are some photographs showing that when Charlie Christian appears to be doing rhythmic strumming he is muting the lowest two bass strings with his thumb and playing the top four strings only, like a tenor guitarist or tenor banjoist. Try these techniques and soon you will find that your articulations will become even more Charlie Christian-like sounding in no time!

CHORD SHAPE ABBREVIATIONS. You have been reading through a lead sheet or piece of sheet music and figured out some workable chord shapes from which to play the melodic line or to begin an improvisation from. How can you notate your chord shape choices directly on the score for future reference?

One way is to use a rubber chord block stamp to imprint the shapes directly on your sheet music/lead sheets. However, sometimes there is not enough room between staves to accommodate that process and/or the imprint may cover some of the chord symbols.

Here is a quick and easy method that you might consider using which is based simply on the name of the chord shape and a superscripted number next to it indicating the fret where the Root of that shape is positioned. For instance, if you are in the key of Eb major you could use the Regular A chord shape at the 8th fret (Root on the third string) or the D chord shape at the 4th fret (Root on the second string) or even the F chord shape at the 11th fret (Root on the first string). Here is what you might notate to remind you of what chord shapes to use: [A8], [D4] or [F11] respectively. If you wanted to work out of the Long A chord shape then I would have marked [LA8]. I suggest that you mark this notation in brackets using a colored pencil so that you don't confuse them with the actual chord symbols used to harmonize the song. The important thing to keep in mind is that the super-scripted number represents the fret where the Root of the chord shape you chose is positioned, not the fret where the lowest note of the chord shape is positioned.

With this outline as a guide you should be able to figure out a similar scheme for naming the remaining chord shapes.

CONCLUSION. While I have not covered all of the techniques Charlie Christian used in his playing I have outlined what I feel are the major "common practice" techniques he pioneered for future generations of jazz guitarists (not to mention rockabilly and early rock 'n roll guitarists). When you have worked your way through all of the various sections of this book on the chord shapes of Charlie Christian you will begin to aurally recognize, through repeated listening of his recordings with Benny Goodman, many of the examples I have presented here.

Remember, famous jazz guitarists like Herb Ellis, Jim Hall and Wes Montgomery all cite Charlie Christian as one of their principal sources of inspiration in their desire to learn to play jazz guitar.

Have fun and happy playing!

Joseph Weidlich
Washington DC
June 2005

Joseph Weidlich [b. 1945] began his formal musical studies on the classic guitar. He moved to Washington, D.C. in 1972, from his native St. Louis, to teach classic guitar. He performed in several classic guitar master classes conducted by notable students of Andres Segovia (i.e., Sr. Jose Tomas [Spain], Oscar Ghiglia [Italy] and Michael Lorimer [U.S.]). He has also played renaissance guitar, renaissance lute, and baroque guitar.

In 1978, he completed research on and writing of an article on *Battuto Performance Practice in Early Italian Guitar Music (1606-1637)*, for the Journal of the Lute Society of America, 1978 (Volume XI). This article outlines the various strumming practices, with numerous examples, found in early guitar methods published in Italy and Spain in the early 17th century. In the late 1970s he published a series of renaissance lute transcriptions for classic guitar, published by DeCamera Publishing Company, Washington, D.C., which were distributed by G. Schirmer, New York/London. The American Banjo Fraternity published an article Joe wrote on James Buckley's *New Banjo Book* [1860] in their newsletter, the *Five-Stringer,* #185, Double Issue, Fall-Winter 2000-01.

The banjo has also been no stranger in Joe's musical life. He began learning folk styles in the early 1960s during the folk music boom, later playing plectrum and classic banjo styles as well. His extensive research in the history of minstrel banjo demonstrates how that style formed the foundation of clawhammer banjo. Alan Jabbour, noted old-time fiddler, musicologist and former long-time director of the Library of Congress' American Folklife Center, has said of Joe's book, *The Early Minstrel Banjo: Its Technique and Repertoire*, that "our understanding of the minstrel banjo in the 19th century is greatly enhanced by the long labors you have devoted to the subject and the fine understanding you have brought to it."

Joe has collaborated with banjo builder Mike Ramsey (Chanterelle Workshop, Appomattox, Virginia) in designing two prototype minstrel banjos based on the dimensions described in Phil Rice's *Correct Method* [1858], as well as similar instruments made by William Boucher in Baltimore in the 1840s.

Also published by Centerstream Publishing are Joe's editions of a flatpicking guitar edition of George Knauff's *Virginia Reels* [1839], believed to be the only substantial extant compilation of nineteenth-century Southern fiddle tunes published in the South prior to the Civil War (which includes songs later featured in the early minstrel shows), *Minstrel Banjo—Brigg's Banjo Instructor* [1855], *More Minstrel Banjo*—Frank Converse's *Banjo Instructor, Without A Master* [1865], *Guitar Backup Styles of Southern String Bands from the Golden Age of Phonograph Recordings*, which features the guitar backup styles of Ernest Stoneman's Dixie Mountaineers, the Carter Family, Charlie Poole and the North Carolina Ramblers, Gid Tanner and the Skillet Lickers, and Jimmie Rodgers, often acknowledged as "the father of country music", *Painless Arranging for Old-Time Country Guitar*, and *Old-Time Country Guitar Backup Basics* (based on commercial recordings of the 1920s and early 1930s).

At Eastman Guitars, our skilled luthiers preserve the time-honored methods of craftsmanship to create fine instruments for today's most discriminating players. All of our Uptown model guitars feature select spruce tops and beautifully figured maple backs, fully hand carved and voiced to produce a rich, balanced acoustic tone. Headstocks, tailpieces, pickguards, bridges and fingerboards are constructed from sumptuous ebony. All metal parts are heavily goldplated.

Our Uptown models are available in 16" and 17" body widths, and can be ordered with or without a cutaway - like the 16" Model 800 AR805-E pictured here. The option of a floating Kent Armstrong designed humbucking pickup provides the warm electric sound that defines mainstream jazz guitar. And, every Eastman Guitar comes in a distinctive, durable J.W. Eastman hard shell fiberglass case.

We take great pride in offering totally handcrafted guitars at a price well within the budget of a working musician.

We still make them like they use to.

HANDCRAFTED GUITARS

www.eastmanguitars.com